WILBERFORCE

Front Cover: From a Water Colour by George Richmond in the Collection at the Palace of Westminster. Reproduced by Kind Permission of Mr Speaker.

WILBERFORCE

The Nation's Conscience

Patrick Cormack

PICKERING PAPERBACKS

ISBN 0 7208 0544 9

Phototypeset by Input Typesetting Ltd., London SW19 8DR
Printed in Great Britain by Richard Clay Ltd., Bungay

TO MR. SPEAKER THOMAS,
another great Christian Parliamentarian,
and a dear friend.

Contents

Foreword

by
His Grace the Archbishop of Canterbury

This year marks the one hundred and fiftieth anniversary of the death of William Wilberforce. To read this judicious and perceptive life is to realise that Wilberforce not only helped to reshape the social conscience of his own generation, but that he continues to speak – with power and relevance – to our own century as well.

For he believed, with a kind of unswerving moral passion, that man's inhumanity to man – so exemplified in the slave trade – was, like evil itself, to be conquered rather than merely condemned. He believed too, unlike most of his parliamentary contemporaries – and unlike most of ours too – that politics should always embrace more than just the art of the possible. Instead, as he reminds us, 'there is a principle above everything that is political'. It is the divine will expressed through the Christian faith and the Christian gospel. It was this alone that constituted what Wilberforce called 'true practical Christianity', a Christianity to be lived rather than merely practised, a Christianity to shape both public policy and private morality. It was this perspective that he brought to the great humanitarian issues of his day.

Many of those issues remain in a world still characterised by social injustice, economic exploitation, moral ambivalence and naked violence. No doubt some of today's Christians who encounter Wilberforce in these pages will be unnerved by his moralizing and embarrassed by his doctrinal certainties. That is perhaps inevitable. But few will deny, and many will envy, his capacity to fuse faith and works into what his epitaph, in Westminster Abbey, calls 'the abiding eloquence of a Christian life'. That life offers us now, as then, an inspiring, and viable, Christian polity for a troubled world.

10 May 1983

Introduction

William Wilberforce was one of the most influential Parliamentarians of all time. Though he never held office his talents and determination, and his deep Christian commitment, commanded the respect of Parliament for nearly half a century, and few lives have so touched those of their countrymen. In an age before mass communication, and when only the minority of the population ever saw a newspaper, the name of William Wilberforce was known throughout the land. In an age before political representation became true democracy he was looked on by many who neither had, nor aspired to, the vote, as their representative. He was at once the conscience and the inspiration of the nation.

All that he achieved he achieved through Parliament. Though wealthy he was not connected to any great political family. He never allied himself to any political faction. He travelled little, and never beyond Europe. But this independent Member, whose greatest motivation was his Christian belief, was so inspired by his vision of the Brotherhood of man that he was able to mould the thinking of a whole generation.

In those days it was not unusual for a young man of wealth and talent to enter Parliament at the age of twenty one, and Wilberforce went to Westminster full of ambition for preferment. But if ever there was a 'born again' Christian it was William Wilberforce. Within a space of five years he had rededicated his whole life to two Christian objectives: the reformation of his own country's morals and the abolition of the slave trade. His success in the second of these two crusades is universally recognised; his

achievements of the first were less tangible, but it is beyond
doubt that he and his company of 'saints' played a major part in
sewing the seeds which blossomed as Victorian morality and
formed the basis of a philosophy which transformed Britain and
influenced the world.

Wilberforce had his critics and was the subject of much controversy in his life, frequently attacked for neglecting social evils
in Britain while campaigning against the slave trade. The knowledge and wisdom of hindsight have inclined some modern
writers to echo the remarks of Wilberforce's often jealous, and
generally far less effective, detractors. Such criticism does not
withstand careful and objective scrutiny. Today, Wilberforce is
rightly and widely honoured as a great reformer who actually
achieved a real victory. The story of his life can still be an
inspiration to the Christian politician.

Some thirty years later after his death John Harford published
his 'Recollections of Wilberforce'. Among the letters he received
was one from Dr Hawkins, the Provost of Oriel College, Oxford,
who talked of his own friendship with Wilberforce and who said
of Harford's book 'I must needs thank you for the pleasure I
have derived from your book: I ought to say profit also; for it is
at least my own fault if I have derived no profit from reading the
story of so good a Christian as your admirable friend.'

This brief life does not seek to supplant or replace the major
histories of the period, nor the notable biographies of Coupland
and Furneaux. It merely seeks to tell the story of his life and to
attempt to answer the question, 'What was he like?' It is my
hope that it will help new readers to recognise what this physically
frail, but spiritually strong, politician achieved against all the
odds; and that it will show that we can still derive some profit
and inspiration from the story of the life of 'so good a Christian.'

I would like to thank my friend and colleague, Sir Peter Mills,
who encouraged me to write this book, and the Librarian and
staff of the House of Commons who have been, as always, un-
failingly helpful. I was very fortunate in having as my Research
Assistant, Sebastian Wilberforce, a descendant of the great William, to whom I am particularly grateful for diligent help and for
compiling the index.

I owe a special thanks, too, to His Grace the Archbishop of Canterbury who has so generously written the Foreword, and to my wife, who typed most of the manuscript.

Westminster   Patrick Cormack
Easter 1983

July 1833

'He is cheerful and serene, a beautiful picture of old age in sight
of immortality. Heard him pray with his family. Blessing and
honour are upon his head.' So read the entry in the diary of one
of the youngest and ablest Members of the House of Commons
on 25 July, 1833. William Ewart Gladstone, Conservative Member for Newark since 1832, had just been to breakfast 'with old
Mr Wilberforce.' Gladstone was on his way to the House of
Commons where he was to make his first important speech.
Though his admiration for the old man was warm, and though
their meeting had been most cordial, it was not a speech of which
Mr Wilberforce would have approved. The Abolition of Slavery
Bill was before Parliament and Gladstone, who came from Liverpool and whose family's wealth had derived in part from the
slave trade, was to urge gradual, rather than immediate, emancipation of those slaves for whom Wilberforce had toiled throughout almost fifty years in Parliament and on whose behalf he had
made his last public speech at a meeting in Maidstone, only three
months before.

It had been a short speech but as he concluded a ray of sunlight
had lit up his face and encouraged him to say, 'The object is
bright before us, the light of Heaven beams upon it, and is an
earnest of success.'

Now, with almost the last rays of sunlight the old man would
see came the firm news of that success. For on Friday July 26th
the Bill for the Abolition of Slavery was approved by the Commons and its passing into law was assured. When he was given

the news Wilberforce rejoiced. 'Thank God that I should have lived to witness the day in which England is willing to give 20 millions sterling for the abolition of slavery.' He could now die happy. He had come to London, to his cousin's house at 44, Cadogan Place, a week before. It was, he would have thought, providential that he should have been so close to the House of Commons, scene of so many of his own great battles and triumphs, at the culmination of his life's work. He was not quite seventy four but he was very frail and very infirm. Small of stature and never strong in body, he had confounded the Doctors for over fifty years. Now, however, he had to be carried into the garden or placed on the sofa to receive Gladstone and his other visitors, and on the Saturday night he became very weak. Throughout Sunday he sank. Much of the time he was unconscious, but on the Sunday night he said to Henry, one of his sons, 'I am in a very distressed state.' 'Yes, but you have your feet on the rock.' The response was typically humble, 'I do not venture to speak so positively; but I hope I have.' Those were his last words. Early on the morning of Monday July 29th he died.

It was eight years since he had retired from the House of Commons, even longer since he had been in the eye of the storm, but though to quote the epitaph on his Memorial,

'In the evening of his days
[he] withdrew from public life and public observation
To the bosom of his family
Yet he died not unnoticed or forgotten by his country.'

Within hours of the news of his death the family had received letters signed by the Duke of Gloucester, the Lord Chancellor, by thirty seven Members of the Lords and nearly a hundred Members of the Commons, urging that he should be buried in Westminster Abbey. The Lord Chancellor declared that 'nearly all the Members of both Houses would have joined, had time allowed.'

It was a unique honour for a man who was not only long out of the public eye but who had never, in almost fifty years in

Parliament, occupied any official position in the Government of
his country.

Both Houses suspended their business to attend his funeral
and to quote, again, from his Memorial in the Abbey, 'The Peers
and Commons of England/With the Lord Chancellor, and the
Speaker, at their head

> Carried him to his fitting place
> Among the mighty dead around
> Here to repose
> Till, through the merits of Jesus Christ,
> His only Redeemer and Saviour
> (Whom in his life and in his writings he had desired to glorify)
> He shall rise at the Resurrection of the just.'

This eloquent epitaph, placed on his memorial statue in the
North Aisle of the Abbey a year later, was almost certainly the
carefully composed work of the young Macaulay. But the gesture
which it recorded was spontaneous and was echoed in the streets
of London. As one of his friends wrote in a letter to his son, 'You
would like to know that as I came down The Strand, every third
person I met going about their ordinary business was in
mourning.'

Perhaps the news was most deeply felt in his native Yorkshire.
There, on 3rd August, the York Herald, recording its 'melan-
choly duty' to announce the death of William Wilberforce
claimed that his was a name, 'with which there is probably
associated more love and veneration than ever fell to the lot of
any civilised individual throughout the civilised globe.' Recording that he had died only after witnessing the triumph of his
cause, the Herald went on, 'His warfare is accomplished, his
course is finished; he kept the Faith. Those who regarded him
merely as a philanthropist, in the worldly sense of that abused
term, know but little of his character.'

On 10th August the Herald gave a detailed account of his
funeral and continued to praise him, 'Thus terminated the mortal
career of as pure and virtuous a man as ever lived. . . .'

The deaths of very few men have occasioned such universal
expressions of loss and gratitude, and such widespread mourning.

Those that have, men like Nelson, Wellington, Gladstone and Churchill, have all been 'public men' in the widest sense, men who held the highest offices and who led the nation at times of great peril. Wilberforce's achievements were, in their way, as great but perhaps the reason for the sense of loss his death caused was best described by the friend who wrote, 'Wilberforce, Sir, is a little creature; he is an ugly creature; but look into his face, hear him speak, and you forget it all; he is the incarnation of love.'

How was it that that 'little creature' who again in the words of the epitaph 'was called to endure great obloquy and great opposition', the son of a rich but nationally unknown merchant, whose entry into Parliament was remarkable but conventional, gradually came to lead a great crusade and capture the affections of the nation?

1

Childhood and Youth

William Wilberforce was born on 24th August, 1759 in 27, High Street, Hull, a fine Jacobean house in the very centre of Hull which had been bought, and extensively modernised, by his grandfather in 1732.

Hull was a prosperous port, ranking in importance with Liverpool and Bristol but, unlike them, depending upon the Baltic rather than the Atlantic trade. The merchants of Hull dealt in timber from Norway, iron from Sweden and traded with the Low Countries and Russia and Prussia. Later in the 18th century Hull became a major whaling port too. The Wilberforces were among the first families of Hull, itself the lively centre of East Yorkshire society.

The dominating figure in Wilberforce's family was his grandfather, the first William, who was twice Mayor of Hull, in 1722 and again in 1740. However, this William was by no means the 'founding father' of the family. According to the Editor of Burke's Peerage the Wilberforces are one of the few families able to trace their ancestry back to Saxon England. Their home for centuries was Wilberfoss, about eight miles east of York and this was the name they bore until the first William changed the spelling, by which time branches of the family were prominent in Beverley, the beautiful Minster town nearby, as well as in Hull itself.

The great William Wilberforce was the son of the first William's second son, Robert. We know little about Robert, save that he was a partner in the family firm, and that he died in 1768 soon after the birth of the third of William's sisters. Two of those girls died in early childhood, and William himself was not expected to survive into manhood for he was a weak and feeble boy, puny and short-sighted.

At the age of seven he was sent to Hull Grammar School where the Headmaster was Joseph Milner, a young man of great scholarship. Milner's younger brother, Isaac, later to be the greatest single influence on William's life, was Usher. Weak as he was his voice was already so impressive that Milner used to put Wilberforce on a table to read to the boys so that, 'his elocution might be a model to the school.'

After the death of his father William was sent to live with Robert's elder brother, also William, who owned houses in St James's Place in London and at Wimbledon. Though both uncle and aunt were always held high in their nephew's affections the school to which they put him in Putney, and where he was a Parlour Boarder, seems to have been remarkable only for the disgusting food, dirty Masters and indifferent teaching.

This period, nevertheless, had a great influence on his life. His aunt was a sister of John Thornton, a leading Evangelical, and she was an ardent follower of George Whitfield, Wesley's companion.

William became such a devout Methodist himself that the family in Hull was alarmed. Methodism was regarded with high suspicion in those early days and the thought of his grandson turning out as a Methodist so appalled the elder William that he threatened to cut him from his will.

He was, therefore, brought back to Hull and sent to Pocklington, his grandfather's old school. Pocklington is a little town at the foot of the Yorkshire Wolds, some twelve miles from York. The school had been founded in 1514 but by the mid 18th century it was a very small, and by all accounts very expensive, establishment of about thirty boys. According to William, 'The Master was a good sort of man and rather an elegant scholar, the boys were a sad set . . . I did nothing there.'

In fact he seems to have acquired the conventional classical education of the period, to have developed a good hand, and to have acquired a strong love of books which remained with him throughout his life, in spite of the constant handicap of short sight.

During his holidays from school he was taken to many social functions in Hull in an endeavour to clear his mind of Methodism. He was remarkably persistent in his faith none the less, as numerous affectionate and pious letters to his aunt and uncle in Wimbledon were to show.

In 1774 old Alderman Wilberforce died at the age of eighty six. He was buried at St Mary's Church, Beverley. William was about to become a very rich young man, therefore, when at the age of seventeen, he went from Pocklington to St John's College, Cambridge in October, 1776. By this time he had been well and truly 'rescued' from Methodism and had both the affluence and the inclination to enjoy all that Cambridge society could offer him, though little inclination to become a scholar.

2

Cambridge

It was a very worldly and, as Wilberforce himself later bemoaned, happy-go-lucky and frivolous young man who went up to Cambridge in 1776. It is a pity, however, to view the young William too closely through the critical eyes of the old. He was in no sense a licentious young man given to wild immorality, but, as yet, his life had no particular serious intent or purpose. He was rich. He was happy. He had a lively mind and enjoyed good company and he went to Cambridge, as other young men of the time went, not as one who had struggled to pass examinations or who was desperate to be a scholar, but as one who wanted to enjoy this next and inevitable part in the education of the young man of fashion of the day.

His own strictures about the company he kept were written with a sense of guilt. They coloured his recollections of what he obviously regarded as a mis-spent youth, but they must not allow us to get either the young Wilberforce or the Cambridge of 1776 out of perspective. He himself was neither more nor less than a normal, though highly entertaining and articulate young man, and Cambridge, though not full of dedicated scholars, was not a place barren of serious scholarship. Though there was far more frivolity than apparent study this was partly because the young men who went there wore their learning very lightly. Most had been extremely well grounded in the classics and if their curriculum is, in our eyes, a restricted one, it was one that most had mastered well.

The new Fellow Commoner at St John's at once attracted

attention by his tiny physique (he was only five feet tall) and his bubbling enthusiasm. The later description of Wilberforce as 'all soul and no body' fitted him well. Although never handsome, he had a face which lit up with happiness whenever he was in animated conversation, and that was nearly always. Throughout his life he had a reputation for quick darting movements with something of a grasshopper mind. In conversation he would leap from subject to subject as the fancy and the company took him. He loved people and he loved good talk. What he lacked was the inclination to pursue a subject or follow a line of argument if he found something else diverting, and he was easily diverted. He was in constant demand as an amusing, high-spirited companion, with a fine turn of wit, a gift for mimicry and a melodious singing voice.

The intensity of the Methodist years was certainly a thing of the past. His mother's and grandfather's rescue attempt had been so remarkably successful, that whenever he looked back to his time at Cambridge he could never do so without what we must regard as an exaggerated remorse, in condemning innocent amusements as terrible sins, and failing to realise that unless he had experienced the froth and frivolity of amiable but aimless youth he would never have experienced the significance of a profound religious conversion.

When he first arrived at Cambridge he was, he tells us, introduced, 'to as licentious a set of men as could well be conceived. They drank hard, and their conversation was even worse than their lives.' This, no doubt, was the really 'fast' set and he rapidly detached himself from them, although moving on to enjoy the company of young men he later regarded scarcely more highly. 'Those with whom I was intimate,' he wrote, 'did not act towards me the part of Christians, or even of honest men. Their objects seemed to be to keep me idle. If ever I appeared studious, they would say to me, "why in the world should a man of your future trouble himself with fagging." ' He does not appear to have neglected their tempting advice. He passed his examinations but was not numbered among the 'Honours Men': 'Mathemetics, which my mind greatly needed, I almost entirely neglected and I was told I was far too clever to require them. Whilst my companions were reading hard and attending lectures, card parties and idle amusements consumed my time.' Encouraged even by his Tutors, he took the line that his innate ability would carry him through and that 'swotting' (or 'fagging') was not necessary.

There were those who took a different line, and a far more serious one. Foremost among them was William Pitt, later to become his great friend and to have the most powerful influence over his early political career. Son of the great Lord Chatham, Pitt had already been at Pembroke College for three years when Wilberforce arrived at St John's although they were the same age. They did not become close friends for Pitt was far more devoted to scholarship and moved in much more serious company than Wilberforce. One serious friend who succumbed to the young Yorkshireman's charms was Thomas Gisborne who had rooms next to his in College. Gisborne spent much time studying but often found himself led astray by Wilberforce. His recollections show that the qualities that always endeared Wilberforce to his friends were already there and that there was, in spite of all the gaiety, a serious man in the making. For Gisborne tells us that it was not only by his wit and social powers but by his talents and kindness that Wilberforce, 'speedily became the centre of attraction to all the clever and idle of his own College, and of the other Colleges'. He was, Gisborne said, 'By far the most agreeable and popular man among the Under Graduates of Cambridge.' He gives a delightful picture of Wilberforce returning late in the evening, after a day of social calls and conviviality, and summoning him to join him to share the Yorkshire pie he always kept in his room by hammering his poker and tongs against the back of the fireplace – or by the melodious challenge of his voice. 'When I did go in he was so winning and amusing that I often sat up half the night with him, much to the detriment of my attendance at lectures next day.' .

Gisborne, the future author of 'Principles of Moral Philosophy' obviously found Wilberforce's company well worth keeping, even if Wilberforce himself showed little serious interest in moral philosophy.

During the vacations he either enjoyed the very lively society of Hull, or he travelled with his mother and sister, or visited friends like William Cookson, Wordsworth's uncle, or Edward Christian, brother of the 'Bounty' mutineer, Fletcher, in the Lake District.

While he was at Cambridge his uncle William, of Wimbledon, died. His death left William even richer than before. He did not need to contemplate having to earn any money when he came down from the university. Instead he could contemplate a career in public life. Inevitably it was to Parliament that he looked. For in those days it was no uncommon thing for a young man to go straight from University to the House of Commons. Indeed some, like Charles James Fox (elected at nineteen) even managed to break the rules and got themselves elected before they were twenty one. Wilberforce became determined in his ambition during his final year at Cambridge, and in the winter of 1779 to 1780 he spent a great deal of time in London, much of it in the Gallery of the House of Commons. There, his frequent companion was William Pitt and it was there that their friendship first developed as they both listened to the debates in the Chamber where Pitt's father had once been the commanding presence. One young man was anxious to maintain a family tradition, the other to begin one. Strangely it was Wilberforce who managed to get elected first.

3

Into Parliament

The 18th century House of Commons abounded with full-blooded characters. It was hardly surprising that anyone who wanted to make his mark in the world aspired there. 'You will be in the House of Commons as soon as you are of age, and you must make a figure there if you are to make a figure in your country' wrote Lord Chesterfield in one of his famous letters to his son in 1749. All ambitious youths centred their ambitions on the small wooden panelled Chamber of St Stephen's in the Old Palace of Westminster: so different from, but much more exciting than, today's dignified Chamber in Barry's magnificent Palace. 'To be out of Parliament is to be out of the world', wrote Admiral Rodney from the West Indies in 1780, 'and my heart is set on being in.'

So, in that same year were set the hearts of the two young Williams, Pitt and Wilberforce. It was a particularly exciting year. As they watched from the Gallery, they heard some of the greatest debates in parliamentary history as Edmund Burke and Charles James Fox argued with passion and eloquence against the Ministry of Lord North for its conduct of the war against the American colonies. It was an issue in which William Pitt took more than a passing interest. His father had striven to prevent the conflict and had made his famous final parliamentary speech on it in the House of Lords just three years before, and then been carried out insensible, never to recover.

The sons of Peers destined from birth to a political life, the country gentlemen who maintained a robust independence from party; those who had made their money and craved a coronet; the great soldiers and sailors and lawyers of the day; the most successful manufacturers and merchants and bankers: these were the men who made up the 18th century House of Commons. Though it was far more a magnet then for those who wanted to make their way in the world, then, as now, it was composed of a more varied cross-section of the idealistic, the ambitious, the venal, the great and the insignificant, than could be found anywhere else.

We can see from contemporary prints what the Chamber of St Stephen's looked like and a German visitor at the end of the 18th century relayed something of the atmosphere that must have fascinated and enticed Wilberforce. 'I now, for the first time, saw the whole of the British nation assembled in its representatives in a rather mean little building, that not a little resembled a Chapel. The Speaker, an elderly man dressed in an enormous wig with two knotted curls behind, and a hat on his head, sat opposite me in a lofty Chair. The Members had nothing in particular in their dress. They even come into the House in their great coats, boots and spurs. It is not even uncommon to see a Member stretched out on one of the benches while others are debating. Some crack nuts, others eat oranges or whatever else is in season. Two shorthand writers sat not far from me and endeavoured to take down the words of the speakers; and thus all that is very remarkable may generally be read in print the next day.'

There was much that was remarkable to report from this assembly to which Wilberforce aspired and in which he was to spend the greater part of his life and perform his most notable public services. But first he had to be elected. In these days before the Reform Act many constituencies had electorates so small that aspiring Members depended on the patronage of a nobleman who controlled the nomination to a 'pocket' or 'rotten' Borough. Wilberforce had no great Patron to whom he could look.

He did, however, come from a town where his family had great influence and where he could use that influence, and some of his considerable wealth, to woo one of the few sizeable electorates in the Kingdom.

Hull had a population of 15,000 and, with something over 1,100 electors, also had one of the largest Borough electorates. Those entitled to vote were the hereditary Freemen of Hull. They were described in an official report in 1834 as 'generally persons in low stations of life and the manner in which they are bribed show how little worthy they are of being entrusted with a privilege from which so many of the respectable inhabitants of the Town are excluded.' Each Freeman had two votes and the recognised price for a vote was 2 guineas, or 4 guineas if the elector agreed to use a 'plumper', and vote for only one Candidate. In addition to this the Candidate would pay the travelling expenses of any non-resident Freeman. That generally worked out at ten pounds if the man came, as most of the absent Freeman did, from London. Contemplating standing for Hull was, therefore, a major and expensive decision, especially as the two sitting Members had notable backers. One, Lord Robert Manners, was uncle to the Duke of Rutland, the other, David Hartley, was the candidate of a number of the great Whig Yorkshire magnates led by the Marquis of Rockingham.

Wilberforce was, however, undeterred. In April, 1780, Lord North's Government was defeated in the House of Commons on Dunning's famous Motion that 'The Influence of the Crown has Increased, Is Increasing and Ought to be Diminished'. Such a defeat did not necessitate a General Election but it was quite obvious that one was likely to be called before the term of the Parliament expired in 1781 and so William Wilberforce set to work to win his voters.

On 24th August, 1780, he held a great ox roasting to celebrate his 'coming of age'. On the very same day Lord North asked George III to dissolve parliament. The campaign began in earnest, and on 11th September the candidates went to the hustings to make their speeches. There was no secret ballot in those days. Candidates were able to see whether their persuasions, financial or otherwise, had worked for each elector declared his vote in public at the Guild Hall.

On 12th September, 1780, it was known that Wilberforce's

charm and persuasive abilities, and the expenditure of something around £8,000 (perhaps a quarter of a million in modern terms) had secured him a remarkable triumph. He had as many votes as the other two Candidates combined. The result was Wilberforce, 1,126; Manners, 673; Hartley, 453. He must indeed have excited a genuine popularity. As one of his supporters wrote to him, 'You have engaged so much popularity in your favour among the Burgesses that, with moderate attention on your part, which you will be well disposed to pay them, it will secure your election for the future.'

There was, however, not a little irony in the result. The man who lost his seat, David Hartley, had been the first Member, in 1776, to move a substantive Motion on the issue of slavery in the House of Commons.

There was another touch of irony about the result in general. Pitt failed to get elected, coming bottom of the poll at the University seat of Cambridge. That was only a temporary set back. His connections were such that Sir James Lowther agreed to the Duke of Rutland's request and presented him with the pocket borough of Appleby so that he could enter the House just a few weeks after his great friend, at the beginning of 1781.

Pitt's career is the most amazing in Parliamentary history. Within twenty months of entering the House he was Chancellor of the Exchequer; by the time he was twenty four he was Prime Minister. He remained in that office longer than any other man, save Walpole. And he remained in it during one of the most crucial and difficult periods in the whole of British history.

It says much for Wilberforce that the friendship fostered in the Gallery remained constant until Pitt's death in 1806. Equally it is hardly surprising that Pitt himself exercised so much influence over his friend and contemporary.

Their friendship is one of the most fascinating and important in our political history. One man held the highest office for many years. The other never held any office at all. And yet each looked to and, to a degree, depended upon the other for a companionship and support that he could not find elsewhere.

In the early years it was Wilberforce who probably gave the most. Pitt, even as a child, stood apart and aloof from most of his contemporaries. At Cambridge, where he was reckoned to have the best mind of his generation, he did not indulge in the youthful pranks and frolics of Wilberforce and his 'set'. To the public, and indeed to most of his Parliamentary colleagues, he was regarded as a cold and aloof figure throughout his life. But with Wilberforce he was different. Wilberforce regarded Pitt as having the finest brain of any man he ever knew, but he also treasured him as one of the wittiest of his friends. With Wilberforce Pitt was able totally to relax. If in those early days he had the greatest influence on Wilberforce's political thoughts, Wilberforce gave him the opportunity to unbend and unwind in a way that few others were ever able to do.

Though Wilberforce was fiercely ambitious and very anxious for office when he first entered Parliament he was, from the first, staunchly independent, and he was, at first, the same carefree, charming, convivial host and companion who had been so popular at Cambridge. He joined all the right London Clubs, White's and Brooks's and Boodles and, together with twenty five of his Cambridge contemporaries, including Pitt, almost set up house at Goosetree's where he and Pitt dined most evenings.

His first speeches were constituency ones. In May 1781 he presented a Petition from Hull against the revenue laws. There is no record of what he said and in December of that year he was rather slapped down after a fairly conventionally patriotic homily on the strength of the Navy, and the shipbuilders of Hull.

In March 1782 Lord North's Government was brought down and he was succeeded by Rockingham. Rockingham seemed to hold Wilberforce in high esteem but his death in July prevented his translating that favour into any form of promotion.

With the death of Rockingham, Shelburne became head of the administration and Pitt, aged twenty three, Chancellor of the Exchequer. No office came to Wilberforce, but he was asked, a mark of real favour, to Second the Address to the Crown on the Preliminaries of Peace with America.

He continued his active social life. He had inherited the house at Wimbledon and there Pitt had a regular room as he liked to escape after a late sitting to the country air. He would order, 'an early meal of peas and strawberries' and indulge in all manner of boyish pranks. On one occasion he shredded a silk hat over a flower bed.

In 1783 Shelburne's Ministry fell over the issue of the Peace Treaty and Pitt resigned. During the summer he and Wilberforce, together with another colleague, Eliott, went to France. They visited Rheims and Paris where they met Louis XIV and Marie Antoinette. Wilberforce found the Queen, 'a monarch of most engaging manners and appearance', but her husband obviously did not impress him; 'A clumsy strange figure in immense boots . . . so strange a being (of the hog kind) it was worth going a hundred miles for the sight of him, especially at boar hunting.'

They had to return when Pitt was summoned home and Wilberforce noted, 'that he was better pleased with his own country than before he left it.'

It was a crucial time in the careers of both young men. The strange political combination of the North/Fox coalition which had held uneasy control since the fall of Shelburne, fell, and Pitt, at the age of twenty four, became Prime Minister. Life was difficult for the youngest First Minister the country had ever had. He was not able to command a majority in the House and depended much upon the private and public support of Wilberforce, now recognized as one of the most promising and accomplished young debaters in the House.

In March Pitt felt confident enough to ask to dissolve Parliament and call a General Election and Wilberforce made a momentous decision too. He decided to stand for the County of Yorkshire, the most prestigious constituency in the land.

4

Member for Yorkshire
and Conversion to Faith

To be Member for Yorkshire in the 18th century was to be Member for the largest constituency in the country and, moreover, the constituency with the largest electorate. The two Yorkshire Members between them represented the whole of the vast County except for York and thirteen, mainly small, older Boroughs. It was they who had to speak not only on behalf of the rural interests but to represent the growing and flourishing new industrial towns like Sheffield and Leeds and Halifax and Bradford, none of which returned a single Member to Parliament.

There were twenty thousand electors in all, and although the influence of the great aristocratic families of Lord Rockingham, the Duke of Norfolk and the Duke of Devonshire, was considerable, there were so many independent country gentlemen and feeholders, so many voters from the industrial West Riding and elsewhere, that a contest was a phenomenally expensive undertaking. That is why in the century before the Reform Bill of 1832 only four Yorkshire elections (1734, 1741, 1807 and 1830) were actually fought out to the final ballot at the hustings. In every other year that there was a General Election Members emerged as a result of bargaining between the various interests. In 1779 there had emerged a new organisation, the Yorkshire Association, which was dedicated to Parliamentary reform and consisted mainly of independent country gentlemen. At the time when Wilberforce conceived his ambition early in 1784 the Association in effect had one nomination and the aristocratic faction, now dominated by Lord Fitzwilliam, nephew of Lord Rockingham, the other.

The ambition itself was incredible in one so new and unconnected as Wilberforce and he had to contend with the added stigma of being of a merchant family. As he himself admitted later in a letter to a friend, 'It was very contrary to the aristocratic notions of the great families of the County to place the son of a Hull merchant in so high a situation.'

Nevertheless he triumphed, and he triumphed as a result of one of the most decisive speeches of his life. In March 1784 a Dissolution of Parliament could obviously not be long delayed and Wilberforce determined to travel to York where the Yorkshire Association had convened a County meeting in Castle Yard for March 25th to carry a Loyal Address to the King, partial to Pitt and hostile to Fox, to whom Lord Fitzwilliam was committed.

Wilberforce had two aims in view, to rally support for his friend and hero in his hour of need, and to advance his own claims to the nomination as Candidate for the County. He knew it was a formidable task for both of the County's Members, Foljambe, who was backed by the Fitzwilliam interests, and Duncombe, the Association's first choice, were determined to stand again.

March 25th, 1784, was a wet and blustery day in York. Standing beneath a wooden canopy, the speakers were sheltered from the worst of the elements, but many in the vast, wet and bedraggled crowd could hear little of what was said. It was not until late in the afternoon that Wilberforce himself took the platform. Few knew who this diminutive young man was but he had that priceless asset, a voice that carried and convinced. As one of the local newspapers reports, 'Mr Wilberforce made a most argumentative and eloquent speech, which was listened to with the most eager attention, and received with the loudest acclamation of all. It was indeed a reply to everything that had been said against the Address; but there was such an exquisite choice of expression, and pronounced with rapidity, that we are unable to do it justice in any account we can give of it.' Among the crowd were James Boswell and Dr Johnson, travelling up to Scotland. Boswell's account is briefer but more evocative than the newspaper's: 'I saw what seemed a mere shrimp mount upon the table; and as I listened, he grew, and grew, until the shrimp became a whale.'

While he was speaking Wilberforce was handed a letter from Pitt telling him that Parliament had been dissolved and that an election was to be held. He broke off to read it and then told the crowd, which had ceased to melt away as he spoke, that the King had, at that very moment, appealed to the nation.

The Address was carried and the various factions returned to their respective tavern headquarters, Wilberforce being hailed as a hero by many members of the Association.

He had not, however, yet won. The whole object was to try and avoid an election with all the expense that it entailed. But in order to do so three things had to happen. First of all it had to be shown that he had significant backing, secondly that he would not be sacrificed in any compromise deal which would preserve Duncombe's position but give the Fitzwilliam faction the other Member, and thirdly, therefore, that if forced into a contest by Fitzwilliam he would be able to command enough money to mount a campaign, and enough votes to win one.

In order to ensure his position in Parliament, therefore, he left York for Hull on March 26th and carried out a hurried canvass there, and on April 1st was elected, though his majority was smaller than before, many of the Hull electors doubtlessly resenting his County ambitions. In those days it was not unusual for a Member to stand for two constituencies (and indeed even today it is still allowed) although if elected for both a Member could, of course, only sit for one.

His return to Parliament assured, Wilberforce now devoted his energies to a canvass throughout the County, having been adopted, along with Duncombe, by the members of the Association who had already raised almost £20,000 towards the cost of an election.

In the event most of the money was not needed for the Association's canvass, and that of their opponents, indicated that over 11,000 votes would be pledged to Wilberforce and Duncombe, whilst only 2,500 seemed absolutely hostile. Faced with this evidence, which obviously agreed with their own canvass, Foljambe stood down, Fitzwilliam bemoaning, 'We were certainly not deserted by the better part of it (the County) but beat by the ragamuffins.'

Ragamuffins or not, on 6th April their opponents withdrew and Wilberforce's diary for 7th reads, 'Up early – breakfasted tavern – rode frisky horse to Castle – elected – chaired – dined York tavern.'

In its way it was almost as remarkable a triumph in Yorkshire as Pitt's had been in the House of Commons and on 8th April the young Prime Minister wrote to his friend from Downing Street to congratulate him on 'such a glorious success.'

Elected without powerful aristocratic connections for such a seat, having proved his prowess at the hustings, just as he had begun to show it in Parliament, William Wilberforce, closest friend of the Prime Minister, himself massively endorsed in the General Election, seemed to stand on the threshold of a great Parliamentary career. One of his greatest strengths was that he was already regarded as above and beyond Party, the creature of no faction.

His only weakness was physical. His health was not good but if that held out, who knew where Boswell's 'shrimp' might finish? Those who prophesied great achievements and distinctions were certainly right, but the manner in which those achievements were attained and those distinctions earned would not have occurred to any of Wilberforce's parliamentary contemporaries in the summer of 1784 as they saw him, easy and assured in manner, still the darling of society, enjoying life to the full as he had done since he first went to Cambridge.

1784 was to see a second decisive event in his life. Intervention in Yorkshire politics was obviously a major step. Asking his former school master to take a tour with him on the Continent could hardly have been regarded as such by anyone, but so it proved.

Wilberforce was planning another tour in France, this time with his mother and his sister and two cousins, and when a friend turned down his invitation he asked the former Usher from Hull

Grammar School, Isaac Milner to go instead. It was a journey that was to change his life.

Isaac Milner was one of the most remarkable scholars and Divines of the 18th century. A boy of precocious talents he was forced to leave his Grammar School in Leeds at the age of ten when his father died, and he was set to work as a weaver. Fortunately his elder brother, Joseph, was able to rescue him. Joseph had, by the kindness of his friends, been sent to Cambridge, and after he had graduated he was appointed Master of Hull Grammar School. He immediately sent for his eighteen year old brother, Isaac, and appointed him Usher. We are told that the young man was found at the loom with copies of Greek and Latin texts by his side.

It was in Hull that Isaac Milner met William Wilberforce for the first time but he did not stay long at the Grammar School. In 1770, when he was twenty, Joseph managed to procure him a sizarship at Queen's College Cambridge. A sizar was a poor scholar who, in return for his education, performed certain menial duties in the College such as serving at table. Isaac spilt the soup one day and vowed that he would abolish the custom if he had the chance. He did, for he eventually became Master of his old College. When he graduated he was Senior Wrangler, that is first in mathematics in the whole University. Indeed he was so far ahead of any rival that the examiners wrote the word 'incomparabilis' by his name. He became a Fellow of his College and was ordained in 1776.

In many ways no man could have been a greater contrast to Wilberforce, and not only in the way he used his Cambridge years. Physically he was huge. Marianne Thornton said that he was, 'the most enormous man that it was ever my fate to see in the Drawing Room.' With his rather uncouth manners and his broad Yorkshire accent, his enormous appetite, and his extraordinary timidity about such things as thunder and lightning, he was a strange companion for the tiny, polished dilettante who had made a name for himself in Parliament. Like Wilberforce he was versatile, but where Wilberforce flitted from subject to subject, he delved and mastered. He was a Fellow of the Royal Society by the time he was twenty six, and he became Professor of Natural Philosophy and of Mathematics. Like Wilberforce too, he was much in demand as a wit. Many thought him the most profound and fascinating conversationalist since Dr Johnson.

Milner and Wilberforce had remained in irregular contact after William's election in 1780, and so it was not a stranger from far off years with whom Wilberforce set out to France on 20th October, 1784. The two men had their own carriage, Mrs Wilberforce and her daughter and two cousins occupying another. They made for Nice, via Lyons, and Avignon. There, in a resort already popular with the English, they passed a pleasant winter, dining with friends and notabilities, including the Duke of Gloucester and his son, and even taking picnics in the mild January weather.

On the way out the talk between the two men had frequently turned on religion. Wilberforce's flippancy had prevented any serious discussions but small events can be decisive in our lives. In Wilberforce's case it was the loan of a book. Just before they began their return journey in February 1785, he borrowed a copy of Philip Dodderidge's 'The Rise and Progress of Religion In The Soul'. Dodderidge, who had died in 1751, had been one of the most influential of the Non-Conformist Divines. His name is little known today, although we still sing some of his hymns such as, 'O God of Bethel', and 'Hark the Glad Sound'. In his time, however, he was a man of great influence and his book was widely read. Milner, himself, when Wilberforce showed it to him, said that it was, 'one of the best books ever written' and suggested they should study it on their journey. This is precisely what they did as they bumped their way along the rutted and ill made roads of France, staying in dirty inns, and eating unspeakably bad food, such as would make any modern Frenchman shudder with horror. They encountered appalling ice and snow and on one occasion it was only Milner's prodigious strength that prevented their small coach from falling over a precipice.

Their conversations on this far from comfortable journey were themselves much more comforting than the rather superficial exchanges which were all that Wilberforce had permitted on the way out. He saw no blinding light. The road to the Channel was not the road to Damascus, but his reading and discussions made a profound impression on him and when he returned he resolved to read and study the Bible seriously.

The change was beginning. It was not particularly noticeable to his friends at this stage. Wilberforce had always maintained an outwardly Christian life. He had attended Church at Wimbledon and been a regular attender at a Chapel in Essex Street when in Town. Indeed his friends looked upon him as rather a religious man. Now, however, he was beginning seriously, if quietly, to question the frivolity of his social life, and was in a rather sober frame of mind at the end of the summer session, having helped Pitt try, in vain, to get a Reform Bill through Parliament. He returned to the Continent when the House rose, again with Milner. This time there was no question of idle chatter. There was serious study in the coach as they read the Greek Testament together. They left the ladies in Nice and went on to Genoa.

Wilberforce was now beginning to examine himself. As he wrote in his diary: 'As soon as I reflected seriously upon these subjects the deep guilt and black ingratitude of my past life forced itself upon me in the strongest colours and I condemned myself for having wasted my precious time and opportunities and talents.'

When they spent some time at Spa, in the Austrian Netherlands on the way back, although he was happy to sing and dance and dine, he would no longer go to the theatre or agree to travel on Sundays.

He returned to Wimbledon in November 1785. Robin Furneaux, his most perceptive modern biographer, remarks on his state of mind at this time. 'He was alone for much of the time and his thought fermented in solitude. His old way of life lay in ruins about him, every achievement, ambition and delight, became worthless and even harmful when seen through his newly opened eyes. The more he brooded the more he became convinced of his own sinfulness in having neglected the mercies of God for so long.' He became obsessed with his past failings and with the need to serve his Maker. His diary at the time is a record of mental self-flagellation.

Feeling the need for a spiritual mentor he wrote to John Newton, Rector of St Mary Woolnoth, in the City, whom he had known in his early Wimbledon days when he had stayed with his aunt and uncle.

Wilberforce's life was touched by a series of remarkable men at this time and no one was more remarkable than John Newton. Today, few who sing "Amazing Grace", "How Sweet the Name of Jesus Sounds" or "Glorious Things of Thee are Spoken" have much idea of their author. He always referred to himself as 'the old African Blasphemer' and no clergyman ever had a stranger life. For many years he was a sea Captain, Master of a slaver. He had himself been, for a time, enslaved by an unscrupulous Master on the African coast. He had undergone his conversion while at sea, although it had not at that stage provoked horror of the trade in which he was engaged. When he gave up the sea he was ordained and settled at Olney in Buckinghamshire, where he became a close friend and companion of the poet, Cowper. It was Newton who convinced Wilberforce that he should not give up his political life, but rather that he should seek to use it to do good. He said in a letter to him sometime later, 'It is hoped and believed that the Lord has raised you up for the good of his Church and for the good of the nation.'

Wilberforce had now, in effect, firmly aligned himself, not with the Methodists, but with their spiritual Brethren who remained in the Church of England, the Evangelicals, men and women who rebelled against the comfortable conventional establishment Christianity of the time.

The prevailing mood within the Established Church of the 18th century was one of sloth and lethargy. Anyone who reads the diaries of Parson Woodforde will get a good idea of how a conscientious country Parson performed his duties. There is little spiritual substance there, although there is much talk of physical nourishment. Many parishes did not even have a Parson Woodforde but merely an absentee Vicar who might condescend to appoint an ill-paid Curate. Dr Johnson is alleged to have told Boswell that he never met a religious clergyman in his life and perhaps the reaction of the nominal Christian in the pew is best typified by Lord Melbourne's comments after hearing an Evangelical sermon. 'Things are coming to a pretty pass when religion is allowed to invade private life.' It was this general attitude that Wilberforce now suddenly conceived to be very wrong. It was necessary, he saw, not to be obsessed with doctrinal trivia, but to lead a Christian life throughout the week; not just to set aside Sunday for nominal observance, listening to elegant sermons which had little relation to the Gospel, but to allow that Gospel to embrace every aspect of life and influence every action.

In November he wrote to a number of friends telling them of his new found faith and determination, and of his dilemma. Some dismissed these letters as being the temporary product of a momentary derangement.

But his greatest friend took him seriously. Pitt wrote a very moving letter to him in return in which he said he could not help expressing the fear that Wilberforce was deluding himself 'into principles which have but too much tendency to counteract your own object, and to render your virtues and your talents useless both to yourself and mankind.' He was not seeking to refute the sincerity of the convert's zeal, but he asked, 'if a Christian may act in the several relations of life, must he seclude himself from all to become so? Surely the principles as well as the practice of Christianity are simple, and lead not to meditation only, but to action.' Pitt urged Wilberforce to discuss the whole matter with him. 'Reflect, I beg of you, that no principles are the worse for being discussed, and believe me that at all events the full knowledge of the nature and the extent of your opinions and intentions will be to me a lasting satisfaction.'

They met and talked for two hours. Pitt was unable to change Wilberforce's resolve but his words must have had some effect in reinforcing Wilberforce's determination to stay in public life and to seek to use his possessions and his influence within the House of Commons to further the Christian cause.

Inevitably the friendship between the two was changed, however, and to some degree strained. Wilberforce told Pitt that he could never again be quite the Party man that he had once been. Though he had never been anything other than independent in his judgement, he now made it absolutely clear that he could never share Pitt's view of politics as being an end in itself. Nevertheless he did remain remarkably true to his friend. Whenever he found himself inclined to vote against him he did it with a very heavy heart. More often than not he continued to vote in the same Lobby, and indeed continued to vote on many issues as a typically independent country Member, supporting the Government of the day almost out of duty. Many of these votes were to engender charges of hypocrisy against him when viewed against his moral crusades, but more of that later.

Although he was still in something of a turmoil there was now no question of his leaving public life or Parliament. He did decide that to keep a house at Wimbledon was an expensive luxury consuming money which ought to be given to better causes, but he was sufficiently at peace with himself when he returned to Yorkshire at the end of the summer session in 1786 for one of his friends, who had been fearful of stories about his 'madness' to say with relief, 'If this is madness, I hope he will bite us all.'

That summer he continued his own rigorous self-examination and became more and more conscious of his accountability to God. He was conscious too of the need to find a cause, a cause to which he could devote his new religious zeal so that he could harness that to the political and practical opportunities membership of the House of Commons gave him. Already he had begun to exercise his mind in this direction. His first attempt at humanitarian reform that summer had been in the promoting of a 'Bill for Regulating the Disposal after Execution of the Bodies of Criminals Executed for Certain Offences, and for Changing the Sentence Pronounced upon Female Convicts in Certain Cases of High and Petty Treason'. But this had come to nought and in any event it was hardly the great moral crusade for which Wilberforce was seeking. The idea for that was not far away.

5

A Cause Embraced

'God Almight has set before me two great objects, the suppression
of the slave trade and the reformation of manners'. It was during
1786, after Wilberforce had overcome the inner struggle following his conversion that those two objects became clear to him.
He then began the crusades which were, together, to dominate
and occupy the rest of his life. 1786 was the year of preparation
and 1787 the year of the launching of both crusades.

After Parliament had risen in the summer of 1786 he spent
some time with his family at Scarborough. He then moved to
Nottinghamshire to stay with his cousins the Samuel Smiths at
Wilford House. He buried himself in his books, reading vora-
ciously all the works of history, philosophy, economics and literature he felt he should have devoured at Cambridge. He would
spend nine or ten hours a day entirely on his own, taking a
solitary breakfast, walking without company, always reading. He
joined his hosts only for dinner, then again for a brief supper
before retiring to bed. In the 18th century it was customary to
dine very much earlier than we do today and to take a fairly
substantial supper later in the evening.

When in company his conversation still sparkled and ranged
across a vast number of subjects, but he was conscious that he
needed something on which to focus his attention. He constantly
tried to discipline himself, learning great passages from the Bible,
and trying to make rules about the ordering of his life, and
quizzing himself in his diary on whether he had matched the
exacting standards he had set himself.

We can get an idea of this self-examination and criticism from a diary entry dated December 1786 – 'I trust I shall better keep than I have done by the resolutions of temperance that I make at this moment: no dessert, no tastings, one thing in first course, one in second. Simplicity. In quality moderate . . . never more than six glasses of wine; my common allowance two or three . . . to be in bed always, if possible, by eleven and up by six o'clock. In general to reform in accordance with my so often repeated resolutions. These are now made in the sight of God, and will, I would humbly hope, be adhered to. I will every night note down whether I have been so or not, and . . . at the end of every week set down on this paper whether in the course of it I have in any instance clearly transgressed.'

If he had not found a cause and if we had merely found his diary and did not know to the contrary from countless contemporaries, we might well write him down as an insufferable prig, and a most crashing bore. But whatever he was Wilberforce was never either a prig or a bore. He always lit up any company he graced. However critical he may have been of himself he was never miserable. He certainly obeyed his Master's injunction 'to fast' (in every sense) in secret.

Both study and fasting took their toll on his frail physique and weak eyes. During the summer of 1786 when he returned to Hull in October one of his friends was alarmed that he was 'so emaciated and altered.' It was here at Hull during this month that he had a letter that was to transform not only his life but the lives of millions in countries he would never see.

For that October he received a letter from Sir Charles Middleton urging that he raise the question of the slave trade in Parliament. Sir Charles Middleton (later Lord Barham) was a Member of Parliament himself and is now acknowledged to have been one of the most distinguished naval administrators in our history. He was known to be an Evangelical and he was the father-in-law of one of Wilberforce's contemporaries and friends at Cambridge, Gerard Edwardes. He, and Lady Middleton, herself a considerable figure in artistic circles and a painter of real competence, made their home at Barham Court at Teston near Maidstone, a truly Christian refuge for those in need of comfort, always keeping a room aside for the sick and the destitute. At Teston too they had installed as their Vicar, James Ramsay, a former naval Chaplain who had become appalled by what he had seen of the slave trade during service in the West Indies.

The Middletons believed that Wilberforce was just the man to take up the cause of abolition and champion it in Parliament. They had become increasingly convinced that it was a cause in urgent need of a parliamentary champion by what they had heard from Ramsay, who had produced two pamphlets on the subject, and by a visitor who had stayed at Teston during the summer of 1786, a young Cambridge clergyman who had won a University prize with his essay on "The Slavery and Commerce of the Human Species". This was Thomas Clarkson, a man destined to devote his life to the abolitionist cause.

Together they had discussed who would be the best Parliamentary champion. Wilberforce would, they were sure, be the ideal choice and so the letter was sent. He replied that he felt, 'the great importance of the subject' but that he thought himself unequal to the task. He promised, however, that he would not 'positively decline it;' and added that on his return to London he would visit Teston and 'consult with Sir Charles and Lady Middleton.'

We have no record of the conversations at Teston but they obviously made a deep impression on him for when he returned to London it was to have further discussions on the trade. Wilberforce was now living within the precincts of Westminster, having put his house in Wimbledon on the market and leased 4, Old Palace Yard, a house opposite the entrance of the House of Lords. It was destined to be 'campaign headquarters' for many years.

Here, early in 1787, he received Clarkson and discussed how best to proceed with abolition. They had regular meetings to which others were invited. Clarkson became utterly convinced that Wilberforce was the man to move for abolition in the Commons and did all he could to persuade likeminded friends to reinforce his pleas. There was a particularly important dinner to discuss the project in March 1787 when Sir Joshua Reynolds and James Boswell were among the guests.

More and more civilised and sensible people were becoming alive to the horrors and inhumanity of the slave trade and on 22nd May, 1787, a Committee for the Abolition of the Trade was formed, with Granville Sharp as its Chairman. Wilberforce was not present but his absence from the committee was quite deliberate for he had by then decided that he would act as its Parliamentary advocate. His decision was taken just ten days before that meeting when, at Pitt's new home at Holwood, near Keston, the Prime Minister convinced Wilberforce, as they sat under an oak tree, that he was indeed the man to take up the cause. He urged him to move a Motion on the slave trade and pledged his own support. The oak tree, known thereafter as the Wilberforce Oak, has now gone, but its stump remains, marked by a plaque.

Though the crusade on which Wilberforce was about to embark would occupy most of his time for the next twenty years the other 'great object' – the reformation of manners – was also occupying much of his thoughts during the winter of 1786 and the early part of 1787.

His conversion had made him acutely conscious not only of the superficial nature of official Christianity but also of the depth of depravity of 18th century society. We look upon it as an age of civilisation and elegance, and indeed, it was, but it was an age of squalor too. Hogarth's engravings do not exaggerate the elements of profanity and debauchery at a time when vast numbers of London's teenagers were involved in prostitution, and when drunkenness was so accepted a part of the social scene that even Pitt was drunk in the House of Commons more than once, and renowned orators like Sheridan and Fox more often. Wilberforce felt most keenly that the best way of dealing with 'that general spirit of licentiousness which is present in every species of vice' was to 'change the hearts of men.' He acknowledged it was difficult and so they should endeavour to 'at least so far remove the obtrusiveness of the temptation, that it may not provoke the appetite, which might otherwise be dormant and inactive.' To remove the temptations to which so many succumbed, laws should be brought in to enforce the keeping of the Sabbath and to forbid such things as duelling and lotteries. Harsh punishments should be prescribed for drunkenness, blasphemy and obscenity.

In order to create the climate where such legislation would be acceptable it was necessary to enlist the support of people in high places who would be prepared to proclaim the need to suppress vice. Thus, in 1787 the Proclamation Society, known later as the Society for the Surpression of Vice, was born.

Many people saw it as a monstrous infringement of individual liberties but the licentiousness of which Wilberforce had become so aware was without dispute destroying countless lives and there was a widespread concern about how the rampant social evils of such things as child prostitution and drunkenness could be defeated. Wilberforce was among those instrumental in obtaining the approval of the King and the Archbishop of Canterbury for an 'official' attack on these problems. On 1st June, 1787, the Proclamation was launched and by the autumn the Society itself was established. Naturally it had the wholehearted backing of the Evangelicals but even relatively worldly statesmen like Pitt and Lord North were worried enough to give it their support.

Wilberforce himself embarked in the autumn of that same year on a specific and practical attempt to bring light into a dark corner of England. He went to the West Country to see Hannah More, one of the celebrated 'Blue Stockings', a group of intellectual women anxious to play a larger role in society than the subservient one expected from women of that period. Wilberforce engaged the interest and concern of Hannah and her sisters in the total degradation and ignorance in which the children of the Mendip miners of the Cheddar Gorge were brought up and Wilberforce promised to give her money if she would seek to found some schools for them.

Thus, by the end of 1787 the enthusiastically active Evangelical was involved in a whole range of good causes. But though his work for such schemes as the Mendip schools is worthy of recognition, and though the general influence of Wilberforce and his fellow Evangelicals on the moral climate of the country can scarcely be over-estimated, whatever criticism might be levelled at some of their methods in a more 'sophisticated' age, the cause which was to dominate his life, and with which his name will ever be associated, was the long and often bitterly fought campaign against the slave trade. That must be the central theme in any brief attempt to tell his story and assess his influence.

6

The Slave Trade

The object to which Wilberforce was to devote most of his energies and talents for the rest of his life was not a new one to him. We do not know when he first became aware of, or interested in, the slave trade. Though Hull was never a slave port he could well have heard stories of the West Indies sugar plantations as a child for a document at Wilberforce House in Hull indicates that the family had an interest in a sugar processing plant on the banks of the River Hull in the mid 18th century. But that is mere speculation. There is a strong family tradition, however, that as a school boy in Pocklington he wrote a letter to a York newspaper condemning the trade, although it does not appear to have been published. What is certain is that in 1780, the year of his election to Parliament, he asked a friend who was travelling to the Caribbean to collect information about the conditions of slaves there in the hope, 'that sometime or other I should redress the wrongs of those wretched and degraded beings.' Perhaps this was as a result of his knowledge that his defeated opponent in the Hull election, David Hartley, had been responsible for putting down a Motion on the subject in the House of Commons in 1776.

Everything he heard about the trade must have convinced him that here was a fitting subject for a Christian politician. After his conversion the appeals of the Middletons, of Thomas Clarkson, and finally, of Pitt himself, must have fallen on very willing ears.

If we are to understand the nature of Wilberforce's struggle, to appreciate just what he achieved, we must realise that he was seeking to convince many perfectly rational and personally decent

men and women that their country did not deserve to be called
civilised whilst it encouraged, or even permitted, the slave trade.
That in itself was no easy task. With all the wisdom amd moral
fervour of hindsight we can protest that no honest Christian could
ever claim either the virtue or the faith and not do all in his
power to stamp out a bestial trade in human beings. But if we
did we would protest too much. Who are we in the 20th century,
which has witnessed more examples of man's inhumanity to man
than all the previous centuries of recorded history put together,
to claim the monopoly of virtue?

And any study of the slave trade must begin by acknowledging
not the social conventions that we take for granted, but the
conventions of the age in which Wilberforce lived. That it was
a brutal age his own first Parliamentary crusade illustrates all too
clearly. For that Bill 'for Regulating the Disposal After Execution
of the Bodies of Criminals Executed for Certain Offences, and
for Changing the Sentence pronounced upon Female Convicts
for Certain Cases of High and Petty Treason' which had been his
first attempt at 'humanitarian' reform had two objectives, both
of which show that Wilberforce himself accepted conventions
which we would not begin to call civilised. The first purpose of
the Bill was to cheat the body snatchers who took corpses from
their graves to sell to doctors and anatomy teachers, by prescrib-
ing that the bodies of all those guilty of capital offences, and not
just murder, should be given for the purpose of medical science.
'Why should not those be made to serve a valuable purpose when
dead, who were a universal nuisance when living?' asked the
Surgeon who had enlisted Wilberforce's support for his cause.
The second purpose of the Bill was to end the practice whereby
women convicted of treason were still sentenced to be burned
after being hanged.

In what he accepted and what he advocated, therefore, Wilberforce was not in all things in tune with what we would regard
as civilised feeling, and nor were all those who profited from, or
even engaged in, the slave trade, evil creatures.

In so far as most educated men in the 18th century thought of
the slave trade at all, they thought of it in purely economic terms
as a perfectly acceptable part of the nation's commerce. They

knew as little of how it was conducted as they knew of how coal was extracted from mines in their own country at the same time. It is always the task of the reformer who sees a great evil to make his genuinely compassionate compatriots as aware as he is of the wrongs they are unwittingly condoning, so that they, too, will feel that they are wholly unacceptable. That was Wilberforce's task and it was a measure of his success that within twenty years of taking up the cause a trade which had been practised and condoned by every civilisation in history was outlawed by the British House of Commons.

Wilberforce himself did not fully comprehend the evil until he had studied the subject. Having studied it he made it his main aim in life to show others what he had learned and to share his revulsion.

To appreciate the magnitude of his success, therefore, we have to understand the trade itself, and to understand it as his contemporaries saw it.

The organised shipping of Negro slaves to the Americas was begun by the Spaniards and the Portuguese in the 16th century. As they, and later other European nations, began to settle in and take an interest in South and Central America and the Caribbean and to be aware of the crops that could be produced there, they realised that their needs for large unskilled labour forces could not be met satisfactorily by the native populations. In the 17th century this need was often met from home. There are few British school children who have not recoiled with horror at the stories of Judge Jeffries sentencing Englishmen to be transported to work in the sugar plantations after the Monmouth Rebellion, for instance. And it was common enough for those who had taken arms against the Government, or who had been convicted of serious crimes, to be sent abroad to serve their sentences in this way. Others were recruited as properly indentured servants.

By the 18th century, however, the need for labour was seen to be so great that those in the plantations and at home felt that the only way it could be supplied was by forcibly taking strong, able-bodied men, used to working in tropical climates, and selling them to those who needed their services. The statesmen of Europe were aware that the Colonies were increasingly important to their prosperity, and if the prosperity of the Colonies themselves depended upon slave labour, then so be it. The slave trade was sufficiently acceptable, and widely enough regarded as lucrative, for one of the most prized Clauses in the Peace Treaty at the end of the war of the Spanish Succession in 1713 to be that which gave the British South Sea Company the right to supply 4,000 slaves a year to the Spanish Colonies. By then not only were Spain and Portugal and Britain involved in the trade, but so was every other maritime power, the French, the Dutch, the Swedes, the Danes, and even the Brandenburghers.

The trade seemed to fit in well with the recognised economic theories of the time and for most of the century it was regarded as an acceptable and thoroughly respectable activity. Many of those who advocated it in Parliament were men of impeccable Christian integrity, as were some of the traders themselves. Wilberforce's mentor, John Newton, 'the old African blasphemer', was, as we have seen, himself converted to Christianity whilst Master of a slaver, and without being at that stage converted to fight against his trade. His attitude was doubtless similar to that of an earlier slave Captain, Thomas Phillips, who wrote of his cargo that they were 'poor creatures, who accepting their want of Christianity and true religion (their misfortune more than fault) are as much the work of God's hands, and no doubt as dear to him as ourselves; nor can I imagine why they should be despised for their colour, being what they cannot help, and the effect of the climate it has pleased God to appoint them.'

Men like Newton and Phillips saw themselves as taking part in a perfectly legitimate branch of commerce and one which, on the face of it, must have been very lucrative. For the ships in the 'triangular trade' were never empty. The normal, but not the invariable pattern, was that they would leave Liverpool or some other European port with textiles and miscellaneous articles which would appeal to African tastes: beads, bangles, and other things. They would sail five or six weeks across to Gambia or some other part of the West African coast. There they would buy, from African suppliers, healthy Negroes whom they would stow on their ships, feeding them twice a day, and sailing for eight weeks to the West Indies or the American coast where the

slaves would be sold. There the ship would be loaded with
tropical produce, generally sugar, before returning to Europe.
Often the round voyage would take a year or more, accounting
for the stops to load and muster cargo.

Life at sea in the 18th century was hard enough for any man
and Masters like Newton and Phillips were well aware that the
dangers to their own crew were as great as to those of the slaves.
That is how they saw it, and that was how most others accepted
it.

And yet the whole system was inimical to true Christian principles. Nothing could conceivably justify the appalling horror of
the 'Middle Passage' as the voyage from Africa to the West Indies
was known. What is more the economic justification for the trade
did not stand up to close and detailed scrutiny. It was the task
of Wilberforce and the abolitionists to expose the horrors and to
reveal the anomalies so that those who could not be moved by
humanitarian arguments might at least acknowledge the force of
the economic ones.

It must not be thought that they were preaching to an entirely
hostile audience. After all there were many Members of Parliament like Charles Middleton and William Pitt, who were anxious
that Wilberforce should take up the cause. And the slave trade
had had its enemies almost since its inception. In England Richard Baxter, the great Non-Conformist preacher, had de-
nounced it in the 17th century and Alexander Pope had
condemned it with elegant derision early in the 18th. John Wesley
was an early opponent, though George Whitfield actually bought
slaves on behalf of a charity in which he was involved. Dr Johnson was another fierce enemy. He once toasted the 'next Negro
revolt in the West Indies', when dining at an Oxford College.

The first great English campaigner, however, was another
Yorkshire man, Granville Sharp. The grandson of an Archbishop
of Canterbury and ninth son of the Archdeacon of Northumber-
land, Sharp inherited talent but no wealth. He was apprenticed
as a linen draper in London and then in 1758 he entered the
Ordnance Department at the age of twenty three. It was whilst
there that he began his anti-slavery campaign. It all began when
he came upon one Jonathan Strong, an abandoned slave who had

been beaten and turned out by his master. The story has a familiar ring to those acquainted with Dicken's "Oliver Twist". Nursed back to health and found a job by Sharp and his brother, Strong was later recognised by his former master who attempted to recapture him.

Sharp was anxious to see Strong's freedom guaranteed. Adept at mastering any subject which came his way, he was horrified to discover that there was in effect no prohibition against slavery in this country, or to prevent fugitive slaves being sought, and others offered for sale, through the columns of the press.

It was Sharp's persistence and his recognition as the champion of the slaves' cause, that led to the famous judgement by Lord Mansfield, the Lord Chief Justice, on 7th February, 1772, that the law of England did not allow one man to enslave another.

It was the same Lord Mansfield who, eleven years later, gave a very different verdict in another case in which Sharp was involved. Sharp came to hear of the English slave ship 'Zong', whose Master had thrown 132 slaves overboard in order to safeguard the damaged ship and its remaining cargo. Mansfield's judgement in this case was that it was 'as if horses had been thrown overboard'.

It was largely as a result of the 'Zong' case that the Quakers formed an Abolition Committee in 1783. Soon the movement had more recruits, the most important of whom, a man whose name will always stand with that of Sharp and Wilberforce in the history of opposition to slavery, was Thomas Clarkson.

In 1784 Dr Peter Peckard, Master of Magdalene College and Vice Chancellor of the University of Cambridge, preached a sermon against the slave trade and subsequently set as the subject for a University essay competition the topic, 'Is it Right to Make Slaves of Others Against their Will?' Clarkson entered for the competition and in order to win immersed himself in studies of the slave trade. Having won the prize he translated his essay from the original Latin into English and in seeking a publisher met John Phillips, a member of the Quaker Abolition Committee. It was as a result of this that he came into contact with Granville Sharp and with James Ramsay, the Rector of Teston, who had been presented to his living by Sir Charles Middleton, and who had himself written two pamphlets on slavery and the slave trade.

Moved by his researches and introductions Clarkson wrote, 'I urged myself that never was any cause, which had been taken up by man in any country or in any age, so great and important; never was there one, in which so much good could be done; never one in which the duty of Christian charity could be so extensively exercised; never one, more worthy of the devotion of a whole life towards it; and that, if a man thought properly, he ought to rejoice to have been called into existence, if he were only permitted to become an instrument in forwarding it in any part of its progress.'

Clarkson henceforth dedicated his own life to discovering and exposing the evils of the trade. Having been one of those who recruited Wilberforce to take the Parliamentary leadership, he supplied him with most of the information on which he was to base his Parliamentary campaign.

At great risk to himself Clarkson visited all the slave ports. He quickly discovered that the slave trade was almost as dangerous to British sailors who indulged in it, as to the slaves themselves. The ships had larger crews than ordinary vessels due to the mortality rate among the crews and the need to guard the slaves. Because of the dangers enlistment was not easy. There was, therefore, a press gang type system in operation known as 'crimping' whereby the Masters of slavers would persuade innkeepers to ply likely recruits with so much liquor that they would be carried off unknowing to their fate or, having become drunk, would be faced with the alternative of jail or the slave ship in order to settle their debts.

Clarkson actually saw 'crimping' going on as he talked to men who had sailed on slavers and who had known the dangers of four or five months on the West African coast where 'epidemical fevers' frequently scourged the crews. Over a fifth of the crews of some 350 Liverpool and Bristol slavers perished between 1784 and 1790 alone.

Clarkson gathered evidence of the dreadful conditions in which the slaves were kept, manacled side by side, the right wrist to the neighbour's left, and the same for the feet. Clarkson discovered one ship, the hold of which was only thirty feet long and which was ten feet wide at its broadest. It carried seventy slaves. He heard evidence too of the merciless beatings of women who refused to sleep with any of the crew.

With Clarkson indefatigable in his researches and Wilberforce now totally convinced that he was called to champion the cause in Parliament, the campaign for the abolition of the slave trade had begun in earnest.

7

The Campaign

The aims of the abolitionists were clearly and concisely set out in 1787, 'Our immediate aim is, by diffusing a knowledge of the subject, and particularly the Modes of procuring and treating slaves, to interest men of every description in the Abolition of the Traffic; but especially those from whom any alteration must proceed – the Members of our Legislature.'

There was some debate in the beginning as to whether the campaign should be directed at the abolition of slavery in general, or the trade in particular. Clarkson tells us that, 'it appeared soon to be the sense of the Committee, that to aim at the removal of both would aim at too much, and that by doing this we might lose all.' It was decided that it would be better, therefore, to concentrate on the trade itself because, 'by aiming at the abolition of the slave trade, they were laying the axe at the very root.' It was also a careful political calculation. Had the attack been on slavery itself, there would have been conflict with the various assemblies in the Colonies over an attack on property rights – rights which were particularly highly regarded in the 18th century. There was the added problem that some feared that suddenly to release vast numbers of slaves would be to let loose, 'an irritated race of beings.' The slave trade, however, was something which the Westminster Parliament had every right to regulate or prohibit.

This did not mean that the members of the Committee accepted slavery as an institution and indeed Granville Sharp made it quite plain that he was unhappy about the compromise.

However, what was wanted was a realistic political target and the general opinion was that the slave trade fitted the bill far more than did the wider issue of slavery. In view of the fact that it took twenty years for the British Parliament to abolish the trade who is to say that the Committee was either wrong or timid in its judgement? Then, as now, politics was the art of the possible.

To make anything possible, however, Parliament had to be won over. Why was it that so many felt that a physically weak and small young man of twenty eight, who had been but seven years in the House of Commons, was the right person to spearhead the campaign? It was not surprising that Pitt should place such confidence in Wilberforce's character and talents. He knew, too, that after Wilberforce's conversion, those talents could never be used in any Ministerial position. Whether Wilberforce, with his staunch independence and his butterfly mind, could ever have settled down to being a successful administrator is highly doubtful. His religious conversion put it entirely out of the question, for the independence had been reinforced by an absolute determination never to compromise his religious principles. The bargaining and cajoling and dealing, and above all the membership of a 'party', though that was a much looser term than it is today, was not for Wilberforce, and Pitt knew it. Pitt knew too that great talents would be wasted if his friend did not have a major cause which he could champion.

What is remarkable is not Pitt's recognition of the abilities and the needs of a friend, but the fact that recognition was already widely shared. People as different as Charles Middleton, who was thirty years Wilberforce's senior, and Thomas Clarkson, the young idealist who was determined to devote his life to fighting the evil, saw in Wilberforce the ideal Parliamentary advocate – an advocate upon whom success would depend.

Wilberforce had indeed succeeded in impressing many people since he became a Member, and especially since his triumph in Yorkshire in 1784. Why was he held in such high esteem? Just what was he like, this young Yorkshire Member who had now dedicated his Parliamentary life to making his country more truly Christian and who saw the abolition of the slave trade as an essential and major part of his mission?

Nothing could disguise the fact that he was, as one admirer put it, 'a figure exceedingly undignified and ungraceful, with a voice that could sometimes degenerate into a whine.' But that voice was itself generally 'sweetly musical beyond that of most men, and of great compass', and the face, although not handsome was 'singularly expressive'. Although no one could hide his physical weakness there was 'little to set on the other side' save the tendency to lapse 'into digression' in his speeches, an inevitable product of his almost too active mind.

After great men die those who write their recollections of them often tend to exaggeration. Sir George Stephen, son of one of Wilberforce's dearest friends and closest allies, wrote in his 'Anti Slavery Recollections', talking of the accounts of Wilberforce that he had read, 'I have never yet seen one that was not more flattering than faithful. Wilberforce was superlatively great because he was superlatively good; in other respects he was a first class man, but by no means a "double first"; flattery is insult to his real excellence.'

In 1787 that goodness and real excellence shone through already to such an extent that the Abolition Committee saw in him one who could be a passionate advocate but who could convince without alienating. They acknowledged him as one who had mastered the art of Parliamentary oratory sufficiently to carry his colleagues with him, and as one whose dogged determination would not allow temporary defeat to deflect him from his goal.

One of his most marked characteristics was his wit. He had, Lord Brougham remarked, 'an exquisite sense of the ludicrous in character.' But his innate kindness did not allow him to use this weapon to make enemies. He had, Brougham said, 'so far disciplined his faculties as to keep in habitual restraint, lest he should ever offend against strict decorum, by introducing light matter into serious discussion, or be betrayed into personal remarks too poignant for the feelings of the individual.' He was, 'fearful of giving the least pain in any quarter, even while heated with the zeal of controversy on questions that aroused all his passions, and more anxious, if it were possible, to gain over rather than to overpower an adversary and disarm him by kindness and the force of reason, or awakening appeals to his feelings, rather than defeat by hostile attack.'

This did not mean that he could not debate with vigour. Even towards the end of his time in Parliament he could be stung to reply. Once he silenced the radical Sir Francis Burdett, who was taunting him as, 'the Honourable and religious Gentleman' with such withering sarcasm that Sir Samuel Romilly remarked that it was, 'the most striking thing I almost ever heard; but I looked upon it as a more singular proof of Wilberforce's virtue than of his genius, for who but he was possessed of such a formidable weapon, and never used it.'

Burke praised his oratory. Pitt said, 'Of all men I ever knew Wilberforce has the greatest natural eloquence.' His fault was that he frequently spoke without adequate preparation and was often, 'at first diffusive' but, 'as he warmed, the mind poured forth so copious a stream of eloquence, that the House, enchanted by his voice and manners and words, hung on his lips with delight.'

That was really the key to his success in Parliament. He understood the House of Commons. He had what one observer called, 'an intuitive discernment of men, and a lively sympathy. These enabled him to catch the temper of the House of Commons. He had learned how to handle that powerful instrument, which vibrates, like an organ, to the master's hand, but jars and creaks and groans when touched by unskilful fingers.' Oratory is very different today but even now only those who can command the House of Commons can ever adequately advance their cause.

Pitt acknowledged that no one understood the House better than Wilberforce. It was a verdict in which Canning concurred, 'If there is anyone who understands thoroughly the tactics of debate, and who knows what will carry the House along with him' it was Wilberforce. He had, we are told, 'every quality of an orator: a voice flexible and musical; action easy and effective, competent knowledge of books, great experience of human life; the tact which deals with men; a tenacious memory rich in facts; a fancy stored with images, and the wit which suggests contrasts.'

The writer of these tributes (J. C. Colquhoun) explains why we cannot fully appreciate Wilberforce's eloquence, for most of his great speeches were made before Parliament's debates were extensively and authoritatively reported. Apparently, 'the way the press dealt with him was summary, though certainly not singular. The reporters disliked his religious views; they sneered at his disinterestedness; so they inflicted the punishment that was within their reach. They drew their sponge across his speeches, or else they jumbled his thoughts and sentences into an unintelligible chaos. If you open the newspapers during the many years that Wilberforce was in Parliament you will find his name in the debates appended to it, but the remarks give you no idea of his speech; they are either a mutilated fragment, or a miserable caricature.'

That peculiar form of censureship still often exercised today by a free press, did not apply so much to his speeches on the slave trade and, in any event, the general view was, as Lord Brougham said, that 'when he stood forward as the leader of the abolition, vowed implacable war against slavery and the slave trade, and consecrated his life to the accomplishment of its destruction, there was every advantage conferred upon the great cause, and the rather that he held himself aloof from party connection.'

One more thing should be stressed before beginning to recount the progress of his campaign. Although he was totally devoted to the cause he was not devoted to it to the exclusion of all else. His other great 'object', the reformation of manners, remained important to him, and so even during the summer of 1787 when he was beginning to plan the strategy for his abolition campaign he was busying himself with work for the Proclamation Society, helping Hannah More with her schools and taking a general interest in all matters he felt a Christian Member should embrace.

As for the campaign itself he realised that it would be the more quickly effective if other countries could be persuaded to abolish the trade as well, for that way those who argued that Britain would be putting herself at a commercial disadvantage would have the ground cut from beneath them. For this reason he supplied William Eden, who was currently negotiating a commercial treaty with France, with information on the trade in the hope that the French would be persuaded to come out against it too. He was not successful there, but he was much more so in discussions with Pitt which led to the Prime Minister's ordering the Privy Council, through its Committee on Trade and Plantations, to investigate the trade and British commercial dealings with Africa. These discussions took place early in 1788 and Wilberforce was so totally involved that he exhausted himself.

He became very ill. He had always suffered from digestive problems and had a particularly difficult time during February and March 1788, suffering from attacks of piles and constipation. He had a high fever and was unable to eat. The Doctors feared for his life. A complete collapse of the stomach was diagnosed and one of his physicians, Dr Warren, gave his opinion that, 'that little fellow with his callico guts, cannot possibly survive a twelve month.'

He retired to Clapham and then went to Bath to take the waters. It was at this time that opium was first prescribed for him and he took it for the rest of his life. It was the only thing that gave him any real relief when he was suffering from particularly debilitating attacks, but his strength of character was such that he never took more than was strictly necessary.

He was still so sick in May 1788 that he had to ask Pitt to move the Motion on Abolition for him. All that Pitt did was to suggest that the matter should be debated during the next session of parliament and no one raised any objections. However, the first real debates on the trade did occur that summer when Sir William Dolben, the Member for Oxford University, appalled by what he had deduced about the conditions aboard the slave ships, having seen some of them refitting on the Thames, introduced the Slave Limitation or, as it was sometimes known, The Middle Passage Bill, the aim of which was to limit, for the period of a year, the number of slaves who could be carried on a vessel. It was in this debate that some of the supporters of the trade actually claimed that the Middle Passage was, 'one of the happiest periods of a slave's life', arguing that the whole system was designed to give them comfort and that any restriction on carrying capacity was entirely unnecessary, and that it would be commercially disastrous.

The Bill succeeded in getting through the Commons without

great difficulty but in the Lords even the Lord Chancellor, Lord Thurlow, was hostile to it. Lord Rodney, the famous Admiral, spoke fiercely against it arguing, as so many Admirals did, that the slave trade was the nursery of British seamen.

Pitt was so incensed that he staked his own future on the success of the Bill and, fairly extensively amended, it did get on to the Statute Books. This was a rather inauspicious beginning for the campaign. If a Bill as modest as Dolben's in its aims, and its duration, could excite such hostility what could Wilberforce and his friends look to when the main issue was joined?

*   *   *   *

It was on the 12th May, 1789, that William Wilberforce first rose to address the House of Commons on the slave trade. He was unwell and had not had time to prepare his speech as fully as he would have wished. Indeed he feared that he might not be able to muster the strength to complete it for he wanted to deal with the whole subject at length and to ensure that his colleagues heard every argument that could be advanced against the trade. His fears were groundless. He spoke for three and a half hours to an attentive House, and although he later complained about the accuracy of the reporting of his speech, what we have gives us a clear enough impression of its quality to realise why it was so highly regarded by his audience. It also enables us to understand how it was that this small, sickly young man, so unprepossessing in appearance, was able to command such affectionate respect in the House. As this speech outlined the case which he was to champion with such vigour for almost twenty years until success was finally achieved, it is well to consider carefully what he said. He began by reflecting on his own inadequacy for the task, 'on the weakness of the advocate who had undertaken this great cause' which made him feel, 'both terrified and concerned.' But because of the encouragement which he had received, 'through the whole course of a long and laborious examination of the question,' he took courage and was determined, 'to forget all my other fears, and I march forward with a firmer step in the full assurance that my cause will bear me out, and that I shall be able to justify, upon the clearest principles, every resolution in my hands, the avowed end of which, is the total abolition of the slave trade.'

He then made it very clear that he appreciated the nature of his audience, of the composition of the House. He refused to discuss the subect, 'with any sort of passion'. 'It is not their passion I shall appeal to – I ask only for their cool impartial reason.' And then he came to a passage which illustrates just how fully he did understand his audience: 'I mean not to accuse anyone, but to take the shame upon myself, in common, indeed, with the whole Parliament of Great Britain, for having suffered this horrid trade that has carried on under their authority. We are all guilty – we all ought to plead guilty, and not to exculpate ourselves by throwing the blame on others; and therefore depre- cate every kind of reflection against the various descriptions of people who are more immediately involved in this wretched business.'

The debate was taking place on a report from the Privy Council into the slave trade, a report which had sought to set out the case for and against but which, in Wilberforce's view, had shown, beyond doubt, that the trade was, 'just such in practice as we know from theory it must be.' He talked about the effect upon Africa and asked his colleagues whether they did not see 'that the slave trade, carried on around her coast, must carry violence and desolation to her very centre? But in a continent just emerg- ing from barbarism, if a trade in men is established, if her men are all converted into goods, and become commodities that can be bartered, it follows that they must be subject to ravage, just as goods are.'

It was a speech not without wit and invective. He mocked those who alleged that few enormities had been practised in Africa, 'because in forty years only two complaints had been made.' An Inquiry from the African Committee into 'whether any foul play prevailed in Africa, is somewhat like an application to the Custom House Officers to know whether any smuggling is going on.'

He dealt at length with the unspeakable horrors of the Middle Passage, 'the most wretched part of the whole subject. So much misery condensed in so little room, is more than the human

imagination had ever before conceived.' He was careful not to
bring personal accusations to bear against any of the Liverpool
merchants, 'I will allow them, nay, I will believe them, to be
men of humanity and I will therefore believe, if it were not for
the multitude of these wretched objects, if it were not for the
enormous magnitude and extent of the evil which distracts their
attention from individual cases, and makes them think generally,
therefore less feelingly on the subject, they would never have
persisted in the trade.'

But he was not prepared to spare his audience some excru-
ciating and agonising details, 'Let anyone imagine to himself six
or seven hundred of these wretches chained two and two, surrounded with every object that is nauseous and disgusting, dis-
eased, and struggling under every kind of wretchedness.' He
scoffed at those who had alleged that the slave ships were
equipped for the comfort and convenience of their human cargo.
'The slaves who were sometimes described as rejoicing at their
captivity are so wrung with misery at leaving their country, that
it is the constant practice to set sail in the night lest they should
be sensible of their departure.' As for stories of their being well
fed and enjoying relaxation on the decks during the Passage, 'the
truth is, that for the sake of exercise, these miserable wretches
loaded with chains, oppressed with disease and wretchedness, are
forced to dance by the terror of the lash, and sometimes by the
actual use of it.' He talked of the high death rate during the
Middle Passage, 'not less than twelve and a half per cent perish
in the Passage. Besides these the Jamaica Report tells you, that
not less than four and a half per cent die on shore before the day
of sale, which is only a week or two from the time of landing.
One third more die in the seasoning, and this in a country exactly
like their own, where they are healthy and happy as some of the
evidence would pretend. The diseases, however, which they con-
tract on shipboard, the astringent washes which are to hide their
wounds, and the mischievous tricks used to make them up for
sale are . . . one principle cause of this mortality. Upon the
whole . . . here is a mortality of about fifty per cent, and this
among Negroes who are not bought unless they are healthy at

first, and unless, as the phrase is with cattle, they are sound in wind and limb.'

He was convinced that 'a trade founded in iniquity and carried on as this was' must be abolished. 'Let the policy be what it might, let the consequences be what they would, I am from this time determined that I would never rest until I have effected its abolition.'

Nevertheless he sought to prove 'by authentic evidence, that, in truth, the West Indies have nothing to fear from the total immediate abolition of the slave trade.' All the arguments for economic necessity were unfounded. 'Though justice be the principle of the measure yet I trust, I shall distinctly prove it to be reconcilable with our truest political interests.' He pointed out that the way in which the slaves were treated itself reduced their effectiveness as workers, and the continued death toll made the achievement of a stable workforce impossible. 'Slaves, considered as cattle, left without instruction, without any institution of marriage, so depressed as to have no means almost of civilisation, will undoubtedly be dissolute, and until attempts are made to raise them little above their present situation, this source of mortality will remain.' Wilberforce was as concerned about the spiritual well-being of these degraded people as he was about their physical condition. If the trade were stopped things would be different, he alleged. 'When the Manager shall know that a fresh importation is not to be had from Africa, and that he cannot retrieve the deaths he occasions by any new purchases, humanity must be introduced . . . births will thus increase naturally, instead of fresh accession of the same Negroes from Africa, each generation will then improve upon the former and thus will the West Indies themselves eventually profit by the abolition of the slave trade.'

He was able to show how even minor improvements in the condition of slaves had led to noticeable increases among the slave population. These arguments notwithstanding, 'I still maintain that the West India planters can and will indemnify themselves by the increased price of their produce in our market; a principle which is so clear that in questions of taxation, or any

other question of policy, this sort of argument would undoubtedly be admitted.'

He then used that ever popular device of Parliamentary oratory, the quotation which makes one's opponents look foolish.
He had, he said, 'in my hand the extract from a pamphlet which
states, in very dreadful colours, what thousands and tens of
thousands will be ruined; how our wealth will be impaired; one
third of our commerce cut off for ever, how our manufacturers
will drop in consequence; our land tax will be raised, our marine
destroyed, while France, our natural enemy and rival, will
strengthen herself by our weakness.' His quotation brought forth
shouts of assent from the House at which we are told, 'Mr
Wilberforce added, "I beg, Sir, that Gentlemen will not mistake
me. The pamphlet from which this prophecy is taken was written
by Mr Glover in 1774, on a very different occasion; and I would
therefore ask the Gentlemen whether it is indeed fulfilled. Is our
wealth decayed? Our commerce cut off? Are our manufacturers
and our marine destroyed? Is France raised upon our ruin? On
the contrary do we not see by the instance of this pamphlet how
men in a despondent moment will picture themselves the most
gloomy consequences, from causes by no means to be
apprehended?" '

With a wealth of detail, aided by a persuasive eloquence and
enlivened often by a fiery invective, Wilberforce went remorse-
lessly on. He dealt with the proposition that the slave trade was
essential to the well-being of the Navy. This, he asserted, was
another false argument. 'Instead of being of benefit to our sailors
as some have ignorantly urged, I do assert it is their grave. The
evidence upon the point is clear; for by the indefatigable industry
and public spirit of Mr Clarkson the muster roll of all the slave
ships have been collected and compared with other trades; and
it appears that in the result that more sailors die in one year in
the slave trade than die in two years of all the other trades put
together.' Clarkson's researches had indeed paid dividends and
Wilberforce drew upon his figures, and upon the evidence he had
gathered, and the depositions he had taken.

He then came to the argument, in his opinion a very weak and
absurd one, 'which many persons, however, have dwelt upon, I

mean, that if we relinquish the slave trade, France will take it up. If the slave trade be such as I describe it, and if the House is still convinced of this . . . we cannot wish a greater mischief to France than that she should adopt it. For the sake of France, and for the sake of humanity, I trust, nay, I am sure, she will not. France is too enlightened a nation to begin pushing a scandalous as well as a ruinous traffic, at the very time when England proves her folly and resolves to give it up.' He was convinced that England's example would be followed but 'if they be bad enough to adopt it, they would have every disadvantage to cope with. They must buy the Negroes much dearer than we; the manufactures they sell, must probably be ours; an expensive floating factory, ruinous to the health of sailors, which we have hitherto maintained, must be set up; and after all, the trade can only serve as a kind of Gibraltar, upon which they may spend their strength, while the productive branches of their commerce must, in proportion, be neglected and starved.'

In many of his more telling passages his strong Christian commitment shone through. Urging his colleagues to 'make such amends as we can to the mischiefs we have done' to Africa, he recalled that just four centuries before Ireland 'used to derive a considerable trade in slaves with this country. But a great plague having invested the country, the Irish were struck with panic, suspecting, I am sure very properly, that the plague was a punishment sent from Heaven for the sin of the slave trade, and therefore abolished it. All I ask, therefore, of the people of Bristol, is that they should become as civilised now as the Irishmen were four hundred years ago. Let us put an end at once to this inhuman traffic, let us stop the effusion of human blood.

'The true way to virtue is by withdrawing from temptation; let us then withdraw from these wretched Africans these temptations to fraud, violence, cruelty and injustice, which the slave trade furnishes. Wherever the sun shines, let us go round the world with him, diffusing our beneficence; but let us not traffic, only that we may set Kings against their subjects, subjects against their Kings, throwing discord into every village, fear and terror into every family, setting millions of our fellow creatures a-hunting each other for slaves, creating fairs and markets for human flesh, through one whole Continent of the world, and under the name of policy, concealing from ourselves all the baseness and iniquity of such a traffic.' He argued for a proper commerce with Africa. He trusted that he had shown that it was good policy for the trade to be abolished but he stressed the policy was not his principle, 'I am not ashamed to say it. There is a principle above everything that is political, and when I reflect on the command that says, "Thou shalt do no murder" believing the authority to be divine, how can I dare to set out any reasoning of my own against it, and when we think of eternity and of the future consequences of all human conduct what is there in this life that could make any man contradict the dictates of his conscience, the principles of justice, the laws of religion, and of God.'

His final plea to his colleagues in the House deserves to be quoted in full: 'Sir, the nature and all the circumstances of this trade are now laid open to us; we can no longer plead ignorance, we cannot evade it, it is now an object placed before us, we cannot pass it; we may spurn it, we may kick it out of the way, but we cannot turn aside so as to avoid seeing it; for it is brought now so directly before our eyes, that this House must decide, and justify to all the world, and to their own consciences, the rectitude of the grounds and principles of their decision. A Society has been established for the abolition of this trade in which Dissenters, Quakers, Churchmen, in which the most conscientious of all persuasions, have all united and made a common cause in this great question. Let not Parliament be the only body that is insensible to the principles of natural justice. Let us make reparation to Africa, so far as we can, by establishing a trade on true commercial principles, and we shall soon find the rectitude of our conduct, rewarded by the benefits of a regular and growing commerce.'

Wilberforce then moved twelve Resolutions for the consideration of the House in which he enumerated the details of the trade and summarized the appalling facts he had sought to give.

Immediately he sat down two Liverpool Members, Lord Penryn and Lord Gascoyne sought, in very short speeches, to accuse him of misrepresentation and mis-quotation, and to prophesy that ruin would indeed be the consequence of abolition.

But then Edmund Burke, himself perhaps the greatest orator of his age, spoke. His tribute to Wilberforce was a moving one. He thought 'the House, the nation, and all Europe under very great and serious obligations to the Honourable Gentleman, for having brought the subject forward in a manner the most masterly, impressive and eloquent. Principles so admirable, laid down with so much order and force, were equal to anything he had ever heard in modern oratory; and perhaps were not excelled by anything to be met with in Demosthenes.'

Pitt and Fox both spoke strongly in Wilberforce's support, Pitt arguing that Britain had the resources to prevent an illegal trade in slaves and Fox condemning 'a trade in human kind, so scandalous that it was to the last degree infamous to let it be openly carried on by the authority of the Government of any country.'

The West Indian interests played for time, arguing that it was important that the House should itself take evidence before coming to such a momentous decision as abolition. It was a plausible argument and sufficient Members were persuaded by it, and by fear of the French taking advantage of British abolition, to ensure that the Bill could not get through that session.

It was not to go through for many sessions after. Almost eighteen years of hard campaigning lay ahead. Every circumstance seemed to conspire against the abolitionists. For this was a time of turmoil in France. Within two months of Wilberforce's speech the Bastille had been stormed and the French Revolution was under way. As it progressed from excess to excess even some of those totally convinced of the force and validity of the abolitionists' argument were alarmed lest their support for any such cause here should give a foothold to those who would stir up a French style Revolution in Britain.

Throughout 1789 and 1790 and 1791 Wilberforce and Clarkson continued to amass evidence, the Slave Committee meeting weekly in Wilberforce's house in Palace Yard, close by Parliament itself. Others were recruited to the cause, including Cowper the poet, and Josiah Wedgwood, who produced a cameo of a Negro in chains, bearing the same inscription as the Abolition Committee's seal, "Am I not a Man and a Brother?"

In the General Election of 1791 Wilberforce was returned

unopposed for Yorkshire, even though he himself feared that he
had been neglecting his constituency duties for the greater cause.
After the election he toured Wales with a friend, Thomas Babington. He, and a mutual friend from Cambridge days, Thomas
Gisborne, were to be important allies and supporters in the difficult years ahead, and it was at their country homes, Babington's
Rothley Temple in Leicester and Gisborne's Yoxall Lodge in
Staffordshire that Wilberforce was to do much of his essential
preparatory reading, and to get what little relaxation he allowed
himself. But though he continued indefatigable, circumstances
were very much against him when he moved the Abolition of the
Slave Trade in April, 1791, for by then there was increasing
concern at the turn of events in France and from the West Indies
there was news of slave rebellions in Dominigue (Haiti), Marti-
nique, and Dominica, rebellions which were blamed on the Abolitionists having excited the passions of the slaves.

Wilberforce entered this next round, fortified by great support
from his friends and by the encouragement of John Wesley who,
in what was perhaps the last letter he ever wrote, in February
1791, said, 'If God be for you who can be against you? . . . be
not weary of well-doing. Go on in the name of God, and in the
power of His might, till even American slavery, the vilest that
ever saw the sun, shall vanish away before it. That He, who has
guided you from your youth up may continue to strengthen in
this and all things is the prayer of, dear Sir, your affectionate
servant, John Wesley.'

In 1791 the abolitionists' cause suffered severe reverses in the
House of Commons. On April 18th Wilberforce moved the Abolition of the Slave Trade in another powerful speech. He repeated
many of the arguments he had so eloquently advanced two years
previously but this time lay great stress on the practical side,
seeking to convince the House that economic ruin would not
follow abolition, and that the Navy did not depend upon this
particular nursery for seamen. In spite of his advocacy the opponents of his Motion maintained their hoary old arguments, one
of them even genially comparing the slave trade with butchery:
neither was a particularly amiable business but for all that a
mutton chop was a good thing!

Fox made a particularly impressive and moving speech, so moving in fact that when he sat down one of the Lancashire Members rose and told the House that he had come to vote against abolition but had been converted to the cause by Fox's oratory. Unfortunately he was in a minority and when the vote came Wilberforce's Motion was defeated by 163 votes to 88. The abolitionists were naturally disappointed but they were not deterred. Over the next year their Committee continued its work. More societies were formed and in some towns there were strong campaigns to give up sugar as a mark of disapproval of the trade. Though bad news continued to come from France and there were further disturbing stories from the West Indies, petitions began to come into Westminster from all parts of the country, urging abolition.

There were many of these on the Table, and there was news too that Denmark had abolished the slave trade, at the time Wilberforce again moved its abolition in April 1792. There were no really new arguments to advance and his speech inevitably lacked the sparkle and inspiration of 1789 but his ardour shone through as he told his colleagues that 'he trusted that time and reflection had convinced them that the trade was as injurious to their interests as it was disgraceful to their feelings; and on this ground he should expect to meet with their support to the Motion which he had to submit.' He desired 'no other language than that of conciliation.' He appealed to those who did treat their slaves well, acknowledging that they 'could not perhaps see how the feelings of others could be so hardened or their conduct so cruel. As it was not to such men that the unhappy slaves had to ascribe their misery, neither should a few instances of mildness seem to atone for the general severity.'

He dealt with those worried by the news of revolts in the Caribbean who argued that the abolition of the slave trade would be the prelude to the premature, as they saw it, abolition of slavery. It was not his design, or that of his friends, he said, 'to effect the immediate emancipation of the Negroes. He was exceedingly sensible that they were in a state far from being prepared for the reception of such enjoyment. Liberty, he considered, was the child, the seed, which sewn in any soil, would shoot into a plant and seldom, indeed, failed to vegetate to maturity.' He dealt with all the arguments yet again, giving further examples of the appalling miseries of the Middle Passage. He named, in particular, one Captain Kimber, who had beaten a pregnant fifteen year old slave girl to death. He extolled the example of Denmark, 'whose commerce could less than ours afford any degree of diminution' but which had 'already rejected the foul intercourse.' It was a noble achievement and should make 'Britain blush to have missed the opportunity of leading the glorious example.' He was followed by a speaker who played on the fears caused by the news of the Negro revolt and who derided the abolitionists cause as 'wild, impracticable and visionary.'

It was in this debate that Pitt made what many considered to be one of his very greatest speeches. This time the Abolitionists had the best of the vote as well as the best of the argument, but they did not have total and immediate victory. An amendment was moved for the gradual abolition of the trade, and finally the House of Commons agreed by 230 votes to 85 that the trade should cease on 1st January, 1796. However, when the Bill went to the House of Lords even these delaying tactics were not considered sufficient. The Lords decided that they should conduct their own enquiry and so the Bill proceeded no further.

Nevertheless this was a crucial debate. From now onwards there was no question of whether the trade should be abolished or not. The Commons had decided, and decided by a convincing majority, that abolition would now come. The only argument was about timing and about means, but that in itself gave the opponents of abolition the opportunity for endless attempts at delay, and for the weaker brethren among those who supported Wilberforce, but not with his passion and conviction, to plead in excuse – that the time was not propitious, or that nothing should be done until the war was over, because, after all, the trade would end someday.

Timidity can always be justified by those who fail to have the courage of their convictions. In 1792, when the news from France was ever more alarming and the association of abolition with 'liberal' causes was being carefully fostered, there seemed good excuse. Even Wilberforce found himself somewhat embarrassed for it was in the summer of 1792 that the French Convention, currently holding sway in Paris, bestowed upon him, and upon Clarkson, the title Honorary Citizen, at the same time as they bestowed it on the revolutionary Tom Paine. It was an honour Wilberforce could have done without. When he brought the question before Parliament again in 1793 he was rebuffed, and rebuffed with a very thin House. His first attempt was defeated by 61 votes to 53 and his second by 31 to 29. In 1794 he carried his Foreign Slave Bill through the Commons, only to see it founder in the Lords.

In March 1796 he suffered a particularly severe reverse when he lost his Abolition Bill on its Third Reading by a mere four votes – 74 to 70, because a number of his supporters were attending a performance of a new comic opera. His distaste for the theatre and other such frivolous pursuits was powerfully reinforced! Then in May he could muster only thirty six supporters for a Slave Carrying Bill, designed to improve conditions aboard the slave ships, and the Bill fell because the House was 'counted out' not enough Members being present to allow it to go forward.

Although he was deeply hurt by his supporters' lack of steadfastness, Wilberforce was in 1796 on the eve of one of the most momentous years of his life, a major Parliamentary force. Not yet forty he was already reckoned by many to be the moral leader of his country and this was not merely because of his work for abolition.

On that front alone his activities had not been confined to the battle in Parliament. He had helped constantly to support and sustain the Abolition Committee and he had given great support, too, to the Sierra Leone project, whereby a new African Colony had been established with Freetown as its capital to provide a home for freed slaves, of whom by this time there were about 14,000 in Britain. It was more than an experiment too for in spite of problems it did succeed. It allowed the abolitionists to argue that Africans could organise themselves in a proper society.

During these same years he continued to work for the Proclamation Society and supported the founding of the Society for the Bettering of Conditions and Increasing the Comforts of the Poor, known as The Bettering Society. He also supported Jeremy Bentham's attempts to promote penal reform.

His most prominent public commitment was one which brought about the brief breach with Pitt. Troubled about the war with France, in December 1794 he clashed with his friend when he sought to argue against Pitt's conduct of the war. It was a breach which caused them both distress. But he was unpopular with the Peace Party too, for whilst opposing Pitt, he nevertheless supported him in his suspension of civil liberties at home and so found himself at odds with those who were totally opposed to Pitt. It was an unhappy period but it did not last long.

In 1795 the two men were fully reconciled again when Wilberforce went to Yorkshire in Pitt's coach to rally the freeholders in support of the Government. He was now convinced there was a real danger to national unity and at a critical time in the country's history he felt that unity must be preserved. Once again he made a speech in the Castle Yard. By all accounts, it must have been as impressive and it was, in its way, as decisive as that which had secured him the nomination for the County eleven years previously.

It was during this time too that his own religious life developed most profoundly. He moved to Clapham where he became the focal point and the most influential member of perhaps the most influential small group of religious men and women ever to be involved in public life. And he formulated his own views on religion in a book which was itself to have as profound an influence as almost any book of the 18th or 19th centuries.

8

Clapham and Practical View

Christianity was the mainspring of Wilberforce's life and of all his political work and for the most crucial years of his great campaign it was at Clapham that he sustained, nurtured and developed his Faith.

At the end of the 18th century, Clapham was a delightful village, set amid green fields. Well away from the bustle of Westminster, it was near enough to be the ideal country retreat for a busy politician. Wilberforce first went there to share a 'chummery' with his friend, Henry Thornton in 1792.

Like Wilberforce, Thornton came from a line of prosperous Hull merchants and the two families were already connected by marriage. The Wimbledon aunt who had had such a strong influence on William's boyhood was a Miss Thornton, half sister of John, Henry's grandfather. The Thorntons had settled in Clapham and bought an estate there and when his father died Henry acquired a large Queen Anne house on the West Side of the Common called Battersea Rise. This was the home he asked Wilberforce to share with him and there they lived for four years until Henry married, when Wilberforce moved to Broomfield, a house that had been built in the grounds.

Henry enlarged Battersea Rise, giving it over thirty bedrooms and adding a magnificent oval library, designed by William Pitt. It soon became the main meeting place of a very remarkable group of men and women who gathered together in Clapham at the turn of the 18th century and who later became known as the 'Clapham Saints' or the 'Clapham Sect'.

All but John Venn, the Rector, were laymen but 'saints' is a
less misleading description than 'sect' for, with one exception,
all were members of the Established Church, and thus in a literal
sense they were not a 'sect' at all, though they were all devout
Evangelicals.

In the history of the Church in England no Parish had ever
exercised such a profound and widespread influence as Clapham
did during the last decade of the 18th century and the first twenty
years of the 19th. The Rector, John Venn, was the son of Henry
Venn, himself one of the leading Evangelical Divines of the 18th
century and a former Curate of Clapham. John came there in
1791 and remained until his death, at the age of fifty four, in
1813. Whilst there he was instrumental in founding the Church
Missionary Society and was involved, with his distinguished pa-
rishioners, in a whole range of religious and philanthropic causes,
particularly abolition. Both Thomas Clarkson and Granville
Sharp were members of the group and so was Zachary Macaulay,
who had become deeply troubled by the miseries of the slaves
when he was Manager of an Estate in Jamaica. Zachary, father
of the great historian, Thomas Macaulay, devoted much of his
life to the campaign against the slave trade and went out to Sierra
Leone in 1793 as Governor of the new free settlement there,
returning in 1799, to settle at Clapham. Another great Clapham
anti-slavery champion was the lawyer James Stephen. He later
became Wilberforce's greatest friend, and married his sister as
his second wife.

Among other notable members of the group was Charles Grant,
a statesman and philanthropist who had made a large fortune in
the service of the East India Company and whose particular
interest was in sending missionaries to India. Charles Simeon,
Vicar of Holy Trinity, Cambridge, and another of the founders
of the Church Missionary Society, was a regular visitor to Clapham and so too were Isaac Milner and Hannah More.

Indian peasants, convicts in Australia, the Greeks who were
struggling for independence, the Haitians, these, and many more
spread throughout the world, in addition to the natives of Africa
and the slaves in the West Indies, all had their friends and
supporters in Clapham. Henry Thornton, like Wilberforce, was

in Parliament, Member for Southwark, having refused to contest Hull because he would not buy votes. So was William Smith, the son of a London merchant, and Member first for Sudbury and then for Norwich. The 'Clapham Members' (James Stephen was briefly in the House as well) exercised considerable Parliamentary influence. They had twenty or thirty regular followers of Evangelical persuasion, men who would always put principle before Party. To quote the great historian, G. M. Trevelyan, they looked 'to the facts of the case and not to the wishes of the Minister.' They were members who 'going into the Lobby required to be supplied with a reason rather than a job.'

Although 'the Saints' were intensely religious, dedicated and devoted Christians in the fullest sense of that term, Clapham was in no sense an oppressive place. We get a very good idea of the atmosphere there from John Colquhoun, a friend of many of them, who described Wilberforce as 'the Prime Minister of a Cabinet of Philanthropists' and who gives an engaging description of him; 'In darts the Member for Yorkshire from the green fields to the south, like a sunbeam into a shady room, and the faces of the old brighten and the children clap their hands with joy. He joins a group of elders, captures up a thread of their talk, dashes off a bright remark, pours a ray of happy illumination and for a few moments seems as wise and thoughtful and as constant as themselves. But the dream will not last and these young eyes know it. They remember that he is as restless as they are, as fond of fun and movement. So on the first youthful challenge, away flies the volatile Statesman. A bunch of flowers, a ball is thrown and away dash, in joyous rivalry, the children and the philanthropist. Law and statesmanship forgotten, he is the gayest child of them all.'

Wilberforce's importance to this group of what he himself always called 'true Christians' cannot be over-emphasised. He was, as James Stephen said, 'the very sun of the Claphamic system.' But for Wilberforce there would never have been a group or sect. If he needed the others to make him what he was, they needed him, 'to make a river from a group of pools.'

Throughout the years of his great campaign, it was to Clapham that Wilberforce retreated from Palace Yard whenever he could, for the spiritual sustenance and comradeship of Battersea Rise. If he was the sun of the Clapham system, Clapham was the centre of his universe, much as he enjoyed travelling to Rothley, or to Yoxall, or to Bath and the Mendips.

His personal religious regime at this time was a particularly strict one. From January 1794 to the middle of 1800 he wrote at the top of every page of his diary lists of what he considered his principal faults – volatility, wandering in prayer, Christianity forgetting, Holy Spirit forgetting, truth erring, humility, self-denial, and many more. His entries reveal constant self-examination and criticism.

He was intensely conscious of the fact that it was not sufficient merely to go to Church and to try and observe the Ten Commandments to be a Christian. From 1789 onwards he frequently considered the idea of writing a book that would be a manual of 'practical Christianity' as he envisaged it. At one stage he dismissed the idea, even listing the reasons why he should not write such a book. It could make him seem over-righteous; it could deter people and have an adverse effect upon his own good works by alienating potential, and even actual, friends and supporters.

These views did not prevail. In April 1797 he produced a book which had an immediate and profound effect, and which continued to exercise a very wide influence well into the first half of the 19th century.

It had a formidable title, "The Practical View of the Prevailing Religious System of Professed Christians in the Higher and Middle Classes in the Country Contrasted with real Christianity". It is hardly surprising that it is always referred to merely as "Practical View". His publishers were not confident of its success and produced only five hundred copies. They sold out within days and within six months five editions and 7,500 copies had been sold. It was translated into many European languages and continued to be reprinted for over a quarter of a century. A newly edited edition has recently been published in Britain and America.

"Practical View" does not make easy reading but it contains so much that is central to an understanding of Wilberforce as a man, and to a full appreciation of his thinking, that no one who is interested in his life and work can afford to neglect this, his only major published work.

In the Introduction Wilberforce explained his main aim in writing the book. He was not actually seeking to convince the sceptic or to answer the arguments of those who opposed the fundamental doctrines of religion but 'to point out the scanty and erroneous system of the bulk of those who belong to the class of orthodox Christians.' He wanted to contradict their 'defective system with a representation of what the author apprehends to be real Christianity.'

He says how concerned he had been to see that many people who professed Christianity had, 'scarcely any distinct knowledge of the real nature and principles of the religion they professed.' No subject could be of more importance for, when this life was closed, 'we must stand before the judgement seat of Christ.'

He was troubled that Christianity was, to most people, a system accepted by society rather than a Faith held by individuals. Most of those who called themselves Christians did so merely because their fathers had done the same. Worse, even those who strove to observe the Commandments of Christianity had little real knowledge of what the faith meant. He was haunted by the fear that Christianity in England would suffer the same fate as it had suffered in France, where ignorance of the Church's fundamental principles had left it quite unable to withstand the onslaught of 'puny assailants.'

Wilberforce felt that Christian principles were not properly taught either in schools or at the universities. We have to remember that the people he was addressing were, by his own definition, of the 'higher and middle classes.' He bemoaned the fact that in most of their homes, 'the Bible lies on the shelf unopened and they would be wholly ignorant of its contents except for what they occasionally hear at Church and from the faint traces which their memories still retain of lessons of their earliest infancy.'

He argued that a knowledge of true Christianity could only be derived by 'vigorous resolution and strenuous diligence, and steady perseverance.' But he was confident 'the diligent perusal of the Holy Scriptures would discover to us our past ignorance.' For him it was a matter of the highest importance that the

discovery should be made for those whom he addressed had great
opportunities but great responsibilities as well. They were responsibilities that were sadly neglected. He saw the professed
Christians of his own days as people who overlooked the corrup-
tion and weakness of the world around them and they were
'continually forgetting the authority of God and were wholly
ungrateful for all their many blessings.'

Wilberforce believed that there was a real force for evil in the
world and that man had to contend with this as well as his own
natural depravity. And yet, 'the grand defect of the bulk of
professed Christians' was that they did not feel encumbered by
sin. What gave Wilberforce particular cause for grief was that
what he called the more decent and moral of his contemporaries
seemed oblivious to real religion as he knew it.

If the conversation turned to religion, 'the utmost that can be
effected is, to bring them to talk of things in the gross. They
appear lost in generalities; there is nothing precise and determi-
nate, nothing which implies a mind used to the contemplation of
its object. In vain you try to bring them to speak on that topic,
which one might expect to be ever uppermost in the hearts of
redeemed sinners. They elude all your endeavours; and if you
make mention of it yourself, it is received with no very cordial
welcome at least, if not with unequivocal disgust. It is at the best
a forced and formal discussion.'

Throughout Wilberforce writes with a total lack of that reserve
and inhibition common to most Englishmen. We may feel that
sometimes, in his burning intensity, he verges on the unbarit-
able, misunderstanding this reserve or inhibition and wrongly
writing it down as indifference. For Wilberforce was totally en-
thusiastic, happy to be publicly declaiming his commitment at
every opportunity. As he saw it, and tried to convince his readers,
one of the glories of Christianity was that it brought 'all the
faculties of our nature into their just subordination and depend-
ence; and so the whole of man may be devoted entire and har-
monious to the service and the glory of God.'

He was quite convinced that lukewarmness in religion was 'the
object of God's disgust and aversion.' The injunction, 'Thou

Shalt Love the Lord Thy God with all Thy Heart' was to Wilberforce precisely that.

Not that passion and enthusiasm were enough. He saw the need to guard against the view that religious affections could be judged 'by a degree of mere animal fervour, by ardours and transports, and raptures.'

For him true commitment was to be judged by the effect and consistency of the influence of Faith in all aspects of life. This was the only standard by which to test the quality of a Christian's religious affections. We know that he himself constantly examined his own conduct and in "Practical View" he tells his readers that we should always be 'impartially examining our daily conduct and often comparing our actual with our possible services.'

One section of the book is devoted to the inadequate ideas of nominal Christians of what was acceptable in God's sight. Nominal Christian's 'can look upon their lives with an impartial eye and congratulate themselves on their inoffensiveness in society, on their having been exempt from any gross vice . . . or on it never having been indulged habitually.' Wilberforce saw the nominal Christian of the 1790's as the Pharisee in the famous parable of the Pharisee and the Publican.

It is a difficult and sometimes uncomfortable book to read, and not merely because it is often difficult to follow the thread of his argument because he goes off at tangents as he often did in his conversation. No, it is uncomfortable as there is no sparing of his readers' feelings. He is absolutely forthright in his assertions as when he says, 'believing in Jesus . . . we must be deeply conscious of our guilt and misery, heartily repenting of our sins and firmly resolving to foresake them; and thus penitently fleeing for refuge to the hope set before us. Our hopes of escape from punishment must be founded entirely on the merit of our crucified Redeemer.'

There is much more in this strain, and there is much too that the modern reader would find very difficult to accept. A man of his time, Wilberforce himself firmly believed that there was an order and structure in society. In this respect he completely accepted the philosophy of 'the rich man in his castle and the poor man at his gate'. But he was mindful too of the rich man and 'the eye of the needle.' He saw the poor as having positive advantages over the wealthy because 'they are far less indisposed to bow down to that preaching from the cross which is to them that perish foolishness, and to them that are saved the power of God and the wisdom of God.' Because the poor were unlikely to be puffed up by the intoxicating fumes of ambition and worldly grandeur, they were far more likely to be able to enter into the straight and narrow way.

Although this acceptance of a far more rigidly stratified society than we are prepared to take for granted falls harshly on our ears there is very much in "Practical View" which speaks as clearly to the 20th century as it did to the 18th. When he writes, 'it seems in our day to be the commonly received opinion, that provided a man admit in general terms the truth of Christianity, and if he be not habitually guilty of any of the grosser vices against his fellow creatures, we have no great reason to be dissatisfied with him, or to question the validity of his claim to the name and consequent privileges of a Christian, he could well be talking to us.

There is an undeviating strictness about his views. He castigates those for whom 'religion can only claim a stated portion of their thoughts and time and fortune and influence . . . the rest is now their own to do what they will with. They have paid their tithes, the demands of the Church are satisfied, and they may surely be permitted to enjoy what they have left without molestation or interference.' For Wilberforce this was a quite unacceptable compromise. For him religion was for all time and for every day. The true Christian was one who would walk by Faith with his mind firmly fixed on the unseen world and the eternal truth. But that did not mean abdication from the world. He had little difficulty in justifying his very public life.

The Christian should never retire from the role which providence had appointed him to fill; he should be 'active in the business of life and enjoying its comforts with moderation and thankfulness. . . . They will be habitually subordinate in his estimation to the objects of more importance.' This attitude could also give a proper resilience because, with his eyes firmly fixed on what was to come, the Christian could endure any set-back in life. It was a philosophy which he was to practise as well as to preach, especially when poverty overtook him towards the end of his life.

Although he constantly insists that a Christian must live every day by his Faith, he stresses the fundamental importance of the Sabbath, when 'we should joyfully avail ourselves of this blessed opportunity of withdrawing from the business and cares of life.' Here again he is advocating something which he constantly practised in his own life. From the time of his conversion he always refused to partake of anything in the nature of amusements on a Sunday, and only very rarely could he be persuaded to travel or to read anything other than the Scriptures.

He speaks, with particular feeling, of the public man to whom 'the desire of human estimation, and distinction, and honour, of the admiration and applause of our fellow creatures' was of great concern. He was himself often accused of enjoying such applause. If he did, the recollection of the enjoyment must have caused him great pain because he is quite adamant that the true Christian should never seek 'worldly estimation and honour. But if it is bestowed upon him he should accept it as present solace and reward to virtue.'

If some passages of the book seem hard and uncompromising there are passages where he displays a particular sensitivity, based quite obviously on personal experience. He writes with feeling when he remarks, 'disappointed hopes, and unsuccessful competitions, and frustrated pursuits sour and irritate the temper. A little personal experience of the selfishness of mankind, damps our generous warmth and kind affections reproving the prompt sensibility and unsuspecting simplicity of our earlier years. Above all, ingratitude sickens the heart and chills and sickens the very life's blood of benevolence.' Christianity always provided the answer, 'if Christianity were generally to prevail; this world, from being such as it is, would become the scene of peace and prosperity.'

Although there is an acceptance of class divisions that would be quite unacceptable to many modern Christians, and although the style in which it is written sometimes makes Wilberforce sound very smug, there is no doubt that this book does express the philosophy of a very good man, a man for whom trùe practical Christianity 'consists in devoting the heart and life to God' and for whom it 'produces that sobriety and loneliness and tenderness of mind, that meekness of demeanour and circumspection of conduct which are such eminent characteristics of the true Christian.'

Throughout, his love of his country shines out as well as love of God. As he saw it, however, the only true hope for Britain was not 'in her fleet and armies, not so much in the wisdom of her rulers, but in the spirit of her people and in the persuasion that she still contains many who, in a degenerate age, love and obey the Gospel of Christ.'

He believed that, as a result of Christian prayer, there might 'here at least be a sanctuary, a land of religion and piety, where the blessings of Christianity might still be enjoyed, and where the name of the Redeemer might still be honoured, where mankind might be able to see what is, in truth, the religion of Jesus, and what are its blessed effects; and whence, if the mercy of God should so ordain it, the means of religious instruction and consolation might again extend to surrounding countries and to the world at large.'

No politician had ever written such a book before, and no politician has ever written such a book since. It is long, very discursive, and in parts very bigoted. Sometimes the bigotry is understandable, as in his condemnation of duelling: 'that excessive valuation of character, which teaches, that worldly credit is to be preserved at ANY RATE, and disgrace at ANY RATE to be avoided'. Sometimes it is less so, as in his total blindness to any good in the Theatre: 'that place which the debauchee inflamed with wine, or bent on the gratification of other licentious appetites, finds most congenial to his state and temper of mind.'

There is never any mistaking the burning sincerity of the man, nor his central message. "Practical View" gives us one of the clearest insights into the thoughts and beliefs of a public man that we have. His contemporaries, so many of whom already held him in the highest regard, seized on it with remarkable fervour. He was inundated with letters and messages of thanks and congratulations from those who said they had derived inspiration and help from it. Burke read it as he lay dying and drew great comfort from it.

It enhanced an already considerable reputation and its influence was to be felt for many years to come, especially during the following decade, one of the most critical in Britain's history, and the most decisive in Wilberforce's life.

9

Wilberforce
1797–1807: A Crowded Decade

1797 was one of the most important years in Wilberforce's life. April 12th saw the publication of "Practical View" and on the very next day he confided to his diary, 'Babington has strongly recommended Miss Spooner for wife for me. We talked about it.'

Most people regarded Wilberforce as a confirmed bachelor. He was thirty seven and in poor health and although he had been greatly attracted to Speaker Addington's sister-in-law in 1789, when she had married another he had said that 'it is very likely that I shall never change my condition; nor do I feel solicitous whether I do or not.'

His name had never been associated with any other woman before then, nor is there any indication that he had ever contemplated marriage since. But now things were to change with extraordinary speed. On the 15th April he met Miss Spooner for the first time. He was obviously immediately captivated by her. His sons suppressed these passages in his diary when they published his life but Robin Furneaux, in his magnificent biography, quotes extensively from them.

Within a week of their first meeting he was writing that 'his heart was gone' and he was impatient to bring one campaign at least to a speedy and triumphant conclusion. He was staying in Bath at the time and on Sunday 23rd April, 'after sad night haunted with Miss Spooner' he prayed and went to the Pump

Room, then, 'much affected and at length I fear too hastily wrote
. . . declaring to Miss Spooner the state of my mind'. He was
obviously in a fever of excited expectation but 'that night I had
a formal, favourable answer – kept awake all night.' Though he
poured into his journal a veritable hymn of praise to the virtues
of this young lady with whom he had fallen so totally and completely in love, he was yet tortured lest he should be in some way
guilty of distorting his Christian priorities. He believed that she
was admirably suited to him and in his journal he confided, 'I
trust that God will bless me; I go to pray to Him. I feel sadly too
absorbed in the love of her, but I trust this will go off by youth.
I believe her to be a real Christian, affectionate, sensible, rational
in habits, moderate in desires and pursuits, capable of bearing
prosperity without intoxication, and adversity without repining.'

Whilst rejoicing in his love, and wrestling with his conscience,
he suddenly had to leave Bath when Pitt sent for him. The war
had taken a turn for the worse. The Fleet had mutinied and an
extraordinary Clergyman called Williams, whom Wilberforce had
befriended but had had to desist from helping because of his
eccentricities and bad conduct, had put about the story that
Wilberforce was inciting the Army to express their grievances
too.

May 1797 was a busy and turbulent time, but Wilberforce was
able to return to Bath by the middle of the month totally convinced that Barbara Spooner was – 'among all women who ever
lived, I believed, qualified to suit me, and I hope I, in some
degree, to suit her'. He would brook no delay in his anxiety to
make her his own and on the 30th May the marriage took place
in Walcot Church near Bath. He was almost thirty eight, she was
twenty.

A portrait of Barbara painted a few years later shows her to
have been an attractive young woman but she must obviously
have had many other qualities to have so charmed and captured
Wilberforce. Henry Thornton thought her pleasing 'rather handsome than otherwise, with character and unquestionably of pious
disposition. Her fortune is small (£5,000) and the family is not
by any means grand, her father being merely a thriving merchant
in the country with a large family.'

It was not a great marriage by the world's standards and those
of Wilberforce's friends who were alarmed at the haste with
which he had taken so profound a step were not entirely unjus-
tified in their misgivings about Barbara's real suitability.

She proved to be a rather difficult woman, constantly worrying
and so bad a housekeeper that friends who came to stay with
them during their marriage almost invariably remarked on the
appalling food, one declaring that he preferred spiders to what
was served up at the Wilberforce table. But Wilberforce himself
was blissfully happy and remained so. Whatever Barbara's faults
they never appeared to distress him unduly, save when he was
anxious over her health or her worries. And she worried about
everything, particularly her health. As her children grew up she
worried about them lest they should be struck down by dread
disease, shipwrecked, poisoned or, perhaps worst of all, seduced
by harlots! She gave the impression that it was being so miserable
that kept her going, and yet Wilberforce never deviated in his
total devotion, believed himself the most blest of men in his
union, and obviously considered his marriage the most fortunate
event of his life. If his private writings are a remotely reliable
guide he lived happily ever after.

If Wilberforce was happy, and he was, and if his sons and
daughters had a stable and good home, and they did, the criticism
of friends, even when expressed from concern, cannot be allowed
much weight. And one has to acknowledge that Wilberforce
cannot have made the easiest of husbands. To spend thirty five
years with a saint is not an undemanding vocation and yet Barbara
never seems to have complained on that score. She had a very
early introduction to Wilberforce's campaigns and causes for their
honeymoon consisted of a tour of the Mendips visiting the Cheddar schools which Wilberforce had endowed and which Hannah
More and her sister, Patty, ran with pious devotion.

The next few years saw Wilberforce actively interested and
involved in a whole range of charitable and philanthropic endeavours, of which the schools were only one. They were not all
without elements of controversy and in 1797 itself, within a
month of his marriage, he was involved in an episode which
shows him in a less than admirable light.

He was always deeply hurt when anyone attacked Christianity and when those attacks were public the hurt could become fierce anger. By 1797 he was as perturbed as most by the excesses of the French Revolution and viewed with profound distaste and disgust the activities of its English admirers and especially the writing of Thomas Paine whose "Age of Reason" was a crude attack on Christianity. This was the same Paine, of course, who had, together with Wilberforce, been made an Honorary Citizen of France.

The Proclamation Society saw Paine's book as a poisonous publication which must, at all costs, be suppressed. They decided to prosecute Williams, the publisher, and engaged the services of the great advocate, Thomas Erskine, for the purpose.

Thomas Williams was a pathetic figure. Most of his small business was concerned with the publication of trivial religious tracts and the only reason he published Paine's book was to try and earn some money. Erskine became so convinced by this that he dropped the case and urged the Society to show mercy. Unfortunately this was advice which neither Wilberforce nor his colleagues felt able to accept, so convinced were they that the public had been endangered by the publication, and so the hapless Williams was sentenced to a year's hard labour and a fine of £1,000. As he was destitute this meant that he was likely to languish in prison for years. In fact he was released after two, but the case is one of the few really jarring notes in the story of Wilberforce and shows that even a very great and good man could allow deep Faith and strong beliefs to nurture bigotry and sanction persecution.

Williams was not the only man who was caused distress at this time by Wilberforce's refusal to deviate from deeply held convictions. Pitt also fell foul of his friend's rigorous and uncompromising attitudes.

In May 1798 Pitt had a fierce altercation with a Radical Member called Tierney whom he accused of sabotaging Britain's defences by his attacks on the administration's war policy. The Speaker judged this an unparliamentary remark and Pitt was ordered to withdraw it. He refused and so Tierney challenged him to a duel. On the 7th May, Pitt went with his Second,

Dudley Ryder, to Kingston Vale where shots were exchanged. No one was hurt but honour was satisfied in the conventionally accepted manner of the time.

When he heard of the incident Wilberforce was horrified. He had spoken out strongly against duelling in "Practical View" believing it to be a totally sinful practice, utterly alien to the laws of God.

He determined to do something to express his condemnation and put down a Parliamentary Motion against duelling. Pitt was beside himself with worry and wrote to Wilberforce pointing out that if the Motion were carried it would carry him away with it. Wilberforce agonized over what to do but eventually decided that Pit was too important to be sacrificed for this particular principle. Writing to him from Broomfield in Clapham, where he had now established his family home, that it was 'his sincere prayer, my dear Pitt, that you may here be the honoured instrument of providence for your Country's good and for the well-being of the civilised world; and much more that you may at length partake of a more solid and durable happiness and honour than this world can bestow.'

Pitt was understandably grateful and relieved. 'I feel your cordial friendship and kindness on all occasions, as well where we differ as where we agree.'

There is no doubt that Wilberforce was totally convinced that Pitt was the man the country needed at the helm at such a difficult time and he was now, for all that he had struggled to advance the cause of peace, totally committed to supporting the war effort.

It was a commitment that was to be responsible for bringing him into further controversies and to be responsible too for much of the criticism directed at him both during his own life and since his death, criticism founded on the accusation that the man who was prepared to struggle for the freedom of Negroes in far away lands was nevertheless prepared to support the suppression of the basic rights of his fellow citizens at home. It is important to understand the context in which Wilberforce acted and in which this accusation was made. Britain stood virtually alone against France. The Revolution had swept away the French monarchy. Thousands of good and decent people had been taken in the tumbrels to the guillotine in the Place de la Revolution. Atheism was established in France and the French army had triumphed over our allies.

There is absolutely no doubt that there were in Britain those who would have liked to follow the French constitutional example, even if not to perpetrate the worst of the French excesses. There were Jacobin Clubs dedicated to the overthrow of the Constitution and among their numbers were those who would have abolished Parliament and established an atheist Republic. Though it is equally true that there were some who were delighted to have an excuse to enact repressive measures to suppress the slightest criticism of the established order of things, Wilberforce was not of their number. And nor were most of those who supported, as he did, what they considered to be necessary restrictions on freedom of expression and action at a time of great national emergency.

It was this shared and general apprehension of the revolutionary forces in society which accounted for the severity with which he treated the Williams case. It was for the same reason that he supported the Habeas Corpus Suspension Act, which enabled the authorities to imprison without trial those who were considered to be a danger to the State.

During the debate on this Act at the end of 1798 a Radical, John Courtenay, complained about the conditions in which a number of people were being held in the prison at Cold Bath Fields. He taunted Wilberforce, saying he was 'certain . . . that the Honourable Gentleman will no longer suffer it to be said by the unfortunate "I was in prison and you visited me not".'

In fact Wilberforce had been there but he had allowed himself to be persuaded that conditions were much better than they were. After an inquiry, when they had been carefully and thoroughly investigated, it appeared that conditions there had indeed been deplorable. Though Wilberforce might have been misled, as were most of his colleagues, over the Cold Bath Fields incident, throughout his public life he consistently supported the cause of penal reform and was counted as a staunch friend by such advocates of reform as Elizabeth Fry, John Howard and Jeremy

Bentham. We cannot castigate him for being less than vigorous in his investigation of one prison scandal without acknowledging his sustained efforts to have some of the most savage penalties on the statute book reduced.

Equally we cannot remark on Wilberforce's support in 1799 for the Combination Law which forbade workers to gather together in unions with their fellows without also acknowledging that he took, throughout his life, the closest and most compassionate interest in the concerns of the poor. The Wilberforce who saw trade unions as a revolutionary threat at a time of national crisis was the same Wilberforce who was prepared to advocate a wealth tax to alleviate the distress of the poor.

There were many specific causes which engaged his sympathy at this time too. In 1800 he was involved in an attempt to outlaw Bull Baiting, and throughout his parliamentary career he supported every attempt to prevent cruelty to animals. Outside parliament his Society for the Suppression of Vice, which had succeeded the Proclamation Society, made animal welfare one of its causes.

He supported an attempt to introduce compulsory vaccination against smallpox. He formed a Society for the Better Observance of the Sabbath. In 1803 he started another one to distribute Bibles. This led, in 1804, to the formation of the British and Foreign Bible Society, of which Wilberforce was a Founder Committee member and Vice President. The Society has an interesting history. It really began in December 1802 when, at a meeting of the Religious Tract Society, the Reverend Thomas Charles, a Methodist Minister from Wales, mentioned the scarcity of Bibles in that country. One of the Committee suggested that a separate Society should be formed to meet not only this need but to cater for the whole country, and indeed the world beyond. Approaches were made to Clapham and ideas were thrashed out at a breakfast at Wilberforce's. It was a cause to which Wilberforce was to become increasingly devoted. The Society appealed to him and to his friends at Clapham because of the powerful support which it gave to their Sunday School movement and because large quantities of Bibles were sent to the missionaries who were supported by the Clapham 'saints' in India, a cause close to Wilberforce at this time. In the first fifteen years of its life the Society was to be responsible for distributing 2½ million Bibles and New Testaments and it continues active today.

From time to time Wilberforce continued to play a crucial role in major national affairs. In February 1801 Pitt resigned, having argued with the King over the question of Catholic Emancipation. Pitt wanted this to accompany the Act of Union with Ireland which brought about the creation of the United Kingdom and in this he had Wilberforce's support. He could not get the Measure through and when he resigned, Wilberforce acted as something of a 'go-between' between Pitt and his successor Addington, the former Speaker. Addington's Ministry was neither long nor glorious and gave birth to the famous rhyme,

Pitt is to Addington,
As London is to Paddington

However, 1801 saw a brief respite in hostilities when the Treaty of Amiens was signed with France. It was obviously a mere truce and although Wilberforce made great efforts to try and prevent a renewal of the war it was inevitable, with Bonaparte now triumphant and determined to dominate Europe, that war would break out again. It did and Pitt returned for his last two years as Prime Minister in 1804.

In 1805 Wilberforce again found himself unhappily at odds with his friends when Lord Melville (formerly Dundas) the Minister in charge of the Navy, was impeached, accused of having misappropriated Government funds. The decision to impeach him was taken on the casting vote of the Speaker. It was said that Wilberforce's speech was decisive, and that had he not taken the line that he did Melville would not have been impeached.

Pitt was obviously deeply distressed both at losing a Minister on whom he placed great reliance and at Wilberforce's playing, as one observer put it, the role of Brutus.

It was even said by some that Wilberforce's action hastened Pitt's end. That is to exaggerate but there is no doubt that it did cause the Prime Minister great grief, and he was increasingly bowed down by the burdens of office. The news of Trafalgar

(October 1805) brought confirmation that Britain enjoyed supremacy at sea, but national rejoicing was muted by Nelson's death and hard on the heels followed the news of the Battle of Austerlitz. This firmly established French superiority on the Continent. 'Roll up the map of Europe, it will not be needed these ten years', Pitt is said to have remarked when the news came. It was too much for him. On 23rd January 1806 he died. He was forty six.

Wilberforce, who helped carry Pitt's banner in the funeral procession in Westminster Abbey was naturally distressed at the loss of his friend, but he was distressed as much by the fact that Pitt had not experienced a religious conversion. Wilberforce told a friend that he had wished many times 'that a quiet interval would be afforded him, perhaps in the quiet evening of life, in which he and I might confer freely on the most important of all subjects.'

Nevertheless Wilberforce showed the depth and strength of his friendship and commitment by busying himself to ensure that Pitt's numerous debts were paid.

Within a year of Pitt's death the cause which he had persuaded Wilberforce to undertake and which he himself had supported consistently but, as the duties of war dominated, with declining vigour, was brought to a triumphant conclusion.

For a decade Wilberforce, despite all of his personal, political and charitable endeavours and involvements, had never ceased to advance the cause of abolition and to give it first place in his priorities. In 1799 an Abolition Motion had been lost by thirty votes and in 1801 a Motion by Canning to limit the trade had been lost also, defeated by a House alarmed by news of new slave revolts. It was in 1801, too, that Wilberforce tried to get a Clause for Mutual Abolition of the Trade inserted into the Treaty of Amiens with France. In 1804 Wilberforce moved the abolition of the trade yet again. The Motion was carried by 124 votes to 49, but again the House of Lords confounded them and he was distressed that Pitt was reluctant to force it through for another year. However, a small legal advance was made when the Privy Council issued an order banning trading in slaves with the captured Colony of Dutch Guiana.

With Pitt's death, however, a new regime came in and Charles James Fox, as Foreign Secretary, was totally committed and enthusiastically determined to see abolition.

The end of the campaign was in sight. Though in 1803 even Wilberforce had been persuaded that he should defer a Motion because of the threat of an invasion, Britain's supremacy at sea was now assured, however strong France might be on the Continent, and there was no reason why all those who espoused the cause should not move forward with proper speed. With Fox as Foreign Minister there was no question of abolition and opposition to the war being mistakenly confused as going side by side.

Although West Indian interests still continued to oppose abolition there was no longer any serious attempt to defend the slave trade in principle. Since the Commons had declared itself in favour of gradual abolition in 1792 and the trade had become regulated as a result of the Limitation Bills, the abolitionists were acknowledged to hold the field and to have won the argument. And yet the trade remained. As late as 1804 the Lords posed so serious a threat to the enactment of abolition that Pitt had felt unwilling to push forward. In 1805 there was even a reverse in the Commons when some of the new Irish Members, whose support had been so important the previous year, succumbed to the West Indian argument that abolition was a threat to property. Nevertheless, the abolitionists pushed in 1805 for partial abolition and saw the order against trade with Dutch Guiana issued in August.

Thus by 1806 the trade had been appreciably reduced and abolition was a cause on which the new Coalition Ministry could unite. On 31st March that year a Bill was brought forward forbidding trade with any captured Colony or foreign power. Wilberforce was able to watch with satisfaction as this Foreign Slave Bill went through both Houses by the 18th May. Grenville, the Prime Minister, and Fox were quite determined to proceed to total abolition and Fox moved a resolution declaring the trade to be 'contrary to the principles of justice, humanity and sound policy'. Wilberforce himself moved an Address to the King urging him to negotiate with foreign powers for the universal abolition of the trade. To frustrate any last minute efforts of the trade lobby another Bill was passed forbidding any non slaving ships from being enlisted in the trade. Wilberforce was able to write that if it 'pleased God to spare the health of Fox and to keep him and Grenville together, I hope that we shall next year see the termination of all our labours'.

His main prayer was to be answered but Fox was not to live to see it. On September 13th 1806 he died. Wilberforce was much effected not so much because Fox had been such a doughty champion of abolition but because, 'he has not one religious friend, or one who knows anything about it. How wonderful God's providence. How poor a master the world!' Wilberforce could only lament Fox's lack of religious faith though he loved him, 'for his generous and warm fidelity to the slave trade cause.' Fox's death was indeed a blow. On his deathbed he had said, 'two things I wish earnestly to see accomplished – Peace with Europe and the Abolition of the Slave Trade. . . . But of the two I wish the latter'. Although he was gone the Ministry remained steadfast.

During the recess Wilberforce turned his thoughts to writing again. The result was, 'A Letter on the Abolition of the Slave Trade; an Address to the Freeholders and Other Inhabitants of Yorkshire'. He had originally envisaged this as a propaganda pamphlet. It became a fairly lengthy exposition of all the arguments against the trade and a detailed answer to all those advanced in its support. It was to prove a powerful tool in the hands of the abolitionists during the final round of their campaign.

It was necessary to have such tools for there was still strong opposition in the Lords. When peers debated the issue early in 1807, the Admirals still spoke out against abolition and so did most of the Royal family, the Duke of Clarence acting as their spokesman on this final occasion. Grenville, appealing to his fellow Peers, spoke with deep feeling about Wilberforce. 'If your Lordships should agree to the abolition of this inhuman traffic in blood . . . it will meet in the other House of Parliament with the strenuous support of the person to whom the country is deeply indebted for having originally proposed the Measure, and for having followed up that proposition by every exertion from which a chance could be derived of success. I cannot conceive any consciousness more gratifying than must be enjoyed by that person, on finding a measure to which he had devoted the labour of his life, carried into effect – a Measure so truly benevolent, so admirably conducive to the virtuous prosperity of this country, and the welfare of mankind – a Measure which will diffuse happiness among millions, now in existence and for which his memory will be blest by millions yet unborn'.

Although there was a vicious and vitriolic attack on Wilberforce by Lord Westmorland, the day was won, a particularly distinguished speech being made by Wilberforce's sole champion in the Royal family, the Duke of Gloucester. At 4.00 a.m. on the morning of February 4th 1807 the Lords voted in favour of abolition.

The Bill came before the Commons on February 23rd. This was to be the crucial day. It was feared that the West Indian interests, falling back upon their arguments of commercial ruin and expediency, could still muster considerable support, but speaker after speaker rose to urge the merits of the Bill and to praise Wilberforce.

The most moving tribute to Wilberforce has passed into parliamentary history. Sir Samuel Romilly concluded, in the words of the Official Report of the debate, 'With an eloquent representation of the gratitude the vote of this night would call forth from prosperity'. Comparing Wilberforce and Napoleon, 'When he looked to the man at the head of the French monarchy, surrounded as he was by all the pomp of power, and all the pride of victory, distributing kingdoms to his family, and principalities to his followers, seeming, as he sat upon his Throne, to have reached the summit of human ambition, and the pinnacle of earthly happiness, when he followed that man into his closet or to his bed, and considered the pangs with which his solitude must be tortured, and his repose banished, by the recollection of the blood he had spilled and the oppressions he had committed: and when he compared with those pangs of remorse, the feelings which must accompany his honourable friend (Mr. Wilberforce) from that House to his home after the vote of that night should have confirmed the objects of his humane and unceasing labours:

when he should retire into the bosom of his happy and delighted
family, when he should lay himself down on his bed reflecting
on the innumerable voices which would be raised in every quarter
of the world to bless him; how much more pure and perfect
felicity must he enjoy in the consciousness of having preserved
so many millions of his fellow creatures, than the man with whom
he had compared him, on the throne to which he had waded
through slaughter and oppression'.

As Romilly sat down the House, in a demonstration such as
had never been seen before, and has never been equalled since,
rose almost to a man to applaud the slight hunched figure whose
moment of triumph had been so movingly described. Wilberforce
was overcome. He wept openly.

His own speech was short but 'distinguished for splendour of
eloquence and force of argument'. When the House divided only
sixteen Members voted against the Bill and 283 voted for it.

It was one of the truly historic moments in parliamentary
history. Though the Bill had to proceed through its Committee
stage success was now assured, and it had its Third Reading on
the 16th March. On the 25th it received the Royal Assent to
become law. From the 1st January 1808 anyone engaging in the
trade would be heavily fined and his ship would be confiscated,
and Britain's naval strength was sufficient to ensure enforcement
of these penalties.

It had been a long and a difficult fight but in retrospect it
seemed to some of his colleagues but a short time since the young
Member for Yorkshire had moved his first Abolition Motion
eighteen years before. As one of his admirers wrote, 'we may
wonder that so much exertion should be necessary to suppress
such a flagrant injustice. The more just reflection will be, that a
short period of the short life of one man is, well and wisely
directed, sufficient to remedy the miseries of millions for ages.'

IO

The Conscience of the Nation

At forty eight Wilberforce was one of the most famous and revered men in Britain. But before the year of his greatest triumph was over he had to fight hard to remain a Member of Parliament.

Since his first triumphant securing of the nomination for Yorkshire in 1784 he had never been forced to go to the polls but in 1807 there were two other Candidates in the field. Both were rich, and neither was prepared to stand down. One, Henry Lascelles, had been his colleague in Parliament, the other was a new Candidate, Lord Milton, son of Earl Fitzwilliam.

There were over 30,000 people entitled to vote in Yorkshire and an election was a prodigiously expensive undertaking. There was deep animosity between the Lascelles and Milton factions, and each tried to claim Wilberforce as his ally. Wilberforce had always been independent. His achievement in Parliament had been gained without his ever belonging to a Party or faction and he was determined to remain aloof from any alliance. This did not prevent his opponents producing elaborate literature claiming his support. The broadsheets claiming 'Wilberforce and Milton for ever' vied with those claiming 'Wilberforce and Lascelles for ever'. His own literature bore the slogan 'Wilberforce for ever'. Rumour and counter-rumour gained ground in Yorkshire. The one that was given most credence was the one that was most damaging to Wilberforce. This alleged that he had broken a pledge of independence to Milton and had secretly allied himself to Lascelles. Lascelles' fortunes owed not a little to the slave

trade and the election rhymes and ballads that were circulated
were, by modern standards inconceivably offensive. One was
headed 'The Monstrous Coalition'.

"We heard of coalitions strange between a Whig and Tory:
But nature sure herself must change ere you believe this story;
What shall the friend of human kind, the advocate of freedom,
Join with the Man whose fetters bind, whose guilty lashes bleed
'em!!
Shall he who purged us from this ill
Join with a Negro dealer
Who of his ever honoured Bill,
Would fain to be the repealer."

And there was more in the same vein, some of it verging on the
obscene.

Wilberforce had real cause to be worried. The Clothiers, for
instance, who had always supported him, were now convinced
that he had joined hands with their enemy Lascelles and so gave
most of their votes to Milton.

In those days polling booths would remain open in a County
for many days and that in York was open for fifteen. Voting was
in public so it was possible to keep a running total of support.
Wilberforce began badly. His opponents, whose purses were
virtually bottomless, had monopolised the transport system, such
as it was, and were bringing in voters from all over the County
and beyond. But Wilberforce's reputation won out. His supporters were not to be deterred. They came in boats and in farm
wagons, and 'even donkeys did the honour of carrying voters for
Wilberforce and hundreds are proceeding on foot'. Friends came,
from London on hearing of his danger.

It was a hard fought contest and a worrying time but he was
able to detach himself from the troubles of the moment and take
comfort from his beliefs. He would go to the Minster in York
and there sit in quiet solitude while outside rival supporters
engaged in heated altercations.

His confidence was justified. The final vote put him top of the
poll. He had 11,806 votes, Milton 11,177 and Lascelles 10,989.
But though he won and though his campaign cost under £30,000

whilst each of his opponents had spent £100,000, it was a close run thing and had there not been a large core of devoted followers who could not be bribed and who were prepared to give their 'plumpers' or single votes to Wilberforce, he could well have been beaten.

As it was, he emerged from the contest confirmed in his position in Yorkshire's affections and he returned to Parliament to carry on his campaign, his prestige increased more than ever by his victory at the polls. His standing in the country and in Parliament was unique. No man before, and no one since, has held quite his position. Unconnected to any great family, belonging to no party or faction, holding no office or official position, he was yet regarded by all as among the foremost men of his time, and by many in Parliament and outside as the living embodiment of the national conscience.

No Minister could afford to ignore his views or advice. He was involved in so much, becoming President or Vice President or Committee member of sixty five societies, and yet he was detached and independent without in any personal sense ever being aloof.

He detached himself too from his old haunts. In 1808 he bought Gore House, Kensington, and set up home there, leaving both Clapham and Old Palace Yard. Though he was not in the forefront of any battle he continued to interest himself in Parliamentary affairs, and in particular to continue to campaign on the slavery issue. He was concerned, for instance, by stories of illegal slave trading and his ambition now was to work towards the total abolition of slavery itself.

His exertions had taken their toll of a never very strong constitution. He developed chest trouble and curvature of the spine, and in 1812 he did not contest Yorkshire at the General Election. He had always taken his duties as Member most assiduously, 'bearing in mind that I am Member for Yorkshire, I own I think it right that I should be present at the agitation of all public questions of the moment, and for the same reason, I should not shrink from the attendance on Committees. . . . I should make all other business bend and give way to that of Parliament. . . . I refuse all invitations for days on which the House sits. I com-

monly attend all the debate instead of going away after the private
business is over for two or three hours, and coming down after
a comfortable dinner; on the contrary I snatch a hasty meal. . . .
I see little or nothing of my family during the session of Parliament. I have stayed until the very end of the session, I believe,
every year for the last twenty three or twenty four.'

Now that he was feeling much frailer and he had a family to
look after and care for he was saddened by the fact that his sons
scarcely knew him. He was particularly upset when one of them
cried when he picked him up and he was told by the nurse, 'He
is always afraid of strangers.' There were six children now, four
boys and two girls, and he thought they had a strong claim on
'a father's heart, eye and voice and friendly intercourse.' He also
felt that as long as he was Member for Yorkshire, 'it will, I fear,
be impossible for me to give my heart and time to the work that
I ought, unless I become a negligent M.P. such as does not
become our great county.'

There was a solution at hand which would allow him to remain
in Parliament, to contribute to debates on the great issues of the
day but to escape the duties which being Member for the first
County in England laid upon him. One of the few virtues of the
unreformed Parliament was that there were constituencies which
imposed no duties on a national figure, where a Member could
be returned because of the interest of a powerful landlord or
Patron. It was a system that had served Pitt well and now it was
to serve Wilberforce. Lord Calthorpe offered him the constituency of Bramber. Because it was entirely within Lord Calthorpe's gift there were many who argued that Wilberforce should
either retire completely or at least seek election to a constituency
which had a proper, if smaller, electorate.

As with most of his decisions he agonised over it and in the
end the pull of family and of Parliament decided him in favour
of Bramber. His duty to his children would come first but he
would not foresake Westminster. In 1812, therefore, William
Wilberforce became Member for Bramber and held the seat until
he finally retired from Westminster in 1825. He still led an active
public life. In spite of his growing infirmity and a religious sense
that was, if anything, stronger than ever, he still felt he could

not 'shut myself up from mankind and immure myself in a cloister. My walk, I am sensible is a public one; my business is in the world; and I must mix in assemblies of men, or quit the post which providence seems to have assigned me.' And there was still much to be done, not least in that first great objective that he had set himself, the reformation of the manners of his country.

He was certainly in a unique position to do things. As one contemporary wrote, 'His sentence was looked for as judgement – the judgement of an impartial mind.' Sydney Smith, we are told, said of him, 'that he could do anything with the House.' Another wrote to him in 1813, 'Your opinion has more weight than that of half the House.'

J. C. Colquhoun observed at this time, 'in the meetings called from time to time for philanthropic purpose . . . he was the undoubted favourite . . . with characteristic simplicity, he used to wonder at the tumult of applause that greeted his appearance and to fancy that the meeting was cheering some remark of the speaker who was then addressing them.' An Italian visitor said of him in 1818, 'When Mr Wilberforce passes through the crowd on the day of the Opening of Parliament, everyone contemplates this little old man, worn with age and his head sunk upon his shoulders, as a sacred relic, as the Washington of humanity.' His power over others was reckoned to be magnetic and 'the secret of its magnetism was its moral purity and its love.'

Colquhoun says, 'Wilberforce had a religious norm of conduct to which he felt he had to conform. But others judged him differently. They, as they watched him, could scarcely believe that human worth could reach so rare perfection. Spirits so buoyant, and yet so self-restrained; a temper so cheerful, yet so even; wit so playful, and yet so innocent; perfection so expansive, and yet so true; a courtesy so uniform, a thoughtfulness so considerate; such reverence for the will of God, yet such charity for man. . . .'

Sir James Mackintosh said that 'when he was in the House of Commons he seemed to have the freshest mind of anyone there, with all the charm of youth about him. He is quite as remarkable in the quiet evening of his days, as when I saw him in his glory many years ago.'

James Stephen, the greatest friend of his later years, and his staunchest friend in the abolitionist cause, was one of those who urged that he should not quit Parliament in 1812. 'Should we lose you before the present difficulties of our case are vanquished, neither my efforts, nor the credit that may be attached to my information are likely to be of any importance.'

When he retired from representing Yorkshire in 1812 he received an Address from the inhabitants of Hull which concluded, 'Amongst other subjects of praise, it is not the least that on retiring from the representation of the County, after a faithful service of twenty eight years, and possessed of the influence which such a station must necessarily command, you have not during that period accepted a place, pension nor rank, and have acquired no other name than the distinguished title of "Friend of Man".'

Wherever he went he was greeted with acclamation. John Harford describes how he went with him to a public meeting of the Freemasons in Clapham in 1814. The meeting had been called to discuss how the Peace Treaty could be amended to serve the abolitionists' cause. He tells us that the room was full to overflowing and that when they arrived, 'the proceedings had already commenced. All the leading Members of the Opposition, including Lords Grey, Holland, and Lansdowne, and Messrs Brougham, Tierney etc. were present. There was also a large attendance of those who are mainly prompted by their benevolent feelings. Mr Wilberforce was recognised as soon as he entered the room, and a lane was quickly formed for him to reach the platform. As we advanced, the meeting began to cheer him; for a few moments he was quite unconscious that he himself was the object of applause, for, walking with his head declined upon his breast he saw no one. As he lent on my arm he whispered to me with perfect simplicity, "Have you caught what is going on?" "They seem to me," I replied, "to be all cheering you. . . .' The moment he was placed in a conspicuous position the whole room rang for some minutes with repeated thunders of applause. In this manner I have seen his presence hailed on many occasions of a public nature, and I cannot conceive it possible for any human being, either at the moment or subsequently, to have been less acted upon by any particle of vanity under such demonstrations of esteem, or rather to have been in a greater degree superior to them.'

He was not merely a hero in his own country. During the peace negotiations in 1814 he was received by both the Tsar of Russia and the King of Prussia. The King of Prussia gave him a set of Dresden china, 'the only thing I ever got by spouting', and he was warmly embraced by the military hero, Marshall Blücher.

In the House of Commons he supported the case of Catholic emancipation and succeeded in having a Clause added to the Charter of the East India Company to enable missionaries to be sent to India.

Not every cause he espoused was popular. He supported the Government over the Corn Law, a measure which kept up the price of bread but which he saw as essential to protect British agriculture. Those who supported the laws were so unpopular that they were frequently attacked and even Wilberforce had a small military guard on his house in Kensington Gore.

He was on the side of the 'oppressors', too, after the Peterloo Massacre. That was the occasion when the Magistrates at Manchester allowed the military to disperse a crowd who had gathered in St Peter's Fields to hear the Radical 'Orator' Hunt. Eleven people were killed in the panic. Fearful that this was the precursor of major civil unrest the Home Secretary of the day, Lord Sidmouth, introduced what came to be regarded as the infamous 'Six Acts'. They included controls on blasphemous literature and public meetings and were regarded by many as unnecessarily repressive. Wilberforce supported the Measures, including the suspension of Habeas Corpus, because he took the threat of revolution seriously.

For the most part, however, his causes were essentially philanthropic. He continued to argue for a humanising of the penal code, he campaigned against the Game Laws and for the chimney boys, and against flogging in the Army. On the very eve of his departure from Parliament he was busying himself in new projects, taking an active interest in the founding of the National Gallery and of the Trustee Savings Bank, and of the Society for the Prevention of Cruelty to Animals.

However, during his last decade in Parliament it was still slavery and the slave trade which continued to occupy most of his attention. In his talks with foreign leaders at the time of the Peace Treaty, in his support of the Negro King of Haiti, Henri Christophe, and in discussions with friends at home and abroad, his constant aim was to see the trade totally eradicated and slavery itself relegated to the history books.

His health, never strong, caused increasing trouble. He was plagued by colitis and weak lungs and in 1821 he asked Thomas Fowell Buxton to take over the leadership of the abolition cause in the House of Commons, feeling himself unequal to the task. When Canning became Foreign Secretary in 1822, after Castlereagh's suicide, Wilberforce again had a close friend in the highest places and he was consulted and given access to secret papers on the foreign slave trade. However, when a Treaty was signed by Britain and the United States acknowledging the trade as piracy the Commons ratified it but the United States Congress did not. Wilberforce believed that Canning had played him false.

In 1822 he was instrumental in founding the Anti-Slavery Society and he published his 'Appeal to the Religion, Justice and Humanity of the Inhabitants of the British Empire on Behalf of the Negro Slaves in the West Indies.'

In March, 1824, he collapsed with pneumonia and although by June he was back in the House he was still very weak. His last speech there was to implore his colleagues not to leave it to the Colonial Governments to alleviate slavery in their territories. Now sixty six, he looked much older than his years and he realised that the time had come when he must resign from Parliament after forty five years of continuous membership. He was offered a Peerage but refused to be ennobled and it was as plain 'Mr Wilberforce' that he retired 'to the bosom of his family' for his last years.

II

The Final Years

Wilberforce's final years were marked by a deep personal contentment and inner happiness which were remarkable in that they accompanied much domestic disruption and distress, and an increasing physical affliction, which together would have broken and embittered most men.

He had always been a moderately wealthy man but he had been so generous throughout his life that money which ought to have been sufficient to guarantee him the most comfortable old age was already so depleted that he had to leave Gore House in Kensington in 1820. For a time he leased Marden Park at Godstone in Surrey and then, in 1822, he moved to Grove House, Brompton Grove, in London. When he retired from Parliament in 1825 he moved to Highwood Hill near Mill Hill where he planned to spend the rest of his life. It was not to be.

During these early years of his retirement he kept in touch with his friends and busied himself in local affairs. He decided to build a Church at Mill Hill, a scheme which was tragically frustrated because the Vicar, another Williams, accused him of being a hypocrite inspired by mercenary considerations. Wilberforce was even driven to publishing a pamphlet defending his position and what should have been a happy episode became a very sad one.

Even sadder was his own financial crisis. Three of his sons, Samuel and Robert and Henry distinguished themselves at Oxford but his eldest son, William, brought about his ruin. Although they remained very close William had always been a trouble to his father. He had to be removed from Cambridge and when he did not persist with his career at the Bar, he drifted into a farming enterprise with a Major Close. It was a disastrous partnership. In 1829 the younger William's losses were so great that he had to go abroad to escape his creditors and his father was totally beggared by the catastrophe, losing some £50,000 – the equivalent in purchasing power of something like 2 million pounds today.

The Wilberforces had to leave Highwood but there was no bitterness; 'What I shall miss most is my books and my garden, though I own I do feel a little for not being able to ask my friends to take a dinner or a bed with me, under my own roof'.

For the last three years of his life Wilberforce stayed with Robert and Samuel, both of whom had been ordained. Samuel was Rector of Brightstone in the Isle of Wight and Robert was Vicar of East Farley in Kent. He did not seem to mind this uprooting in his old age, 'Has not my dear Mrs W and myself great cause for thankfulness, in being moored in our latter days in the peaceful haven which we enjoy (after all my homes during my long and stormy voyage in the sea of politics) under the roofs of our sons in Kent and the Isle of Wight, relieved from all the worries of family cares'.

He delighted in hearing his sons preach and although he tended to fall asleep there is an exchanting account of how he would climb up in his front pew as Sam began to preach, and lean over the pulpit gazing through an eyeglass a few inches away, beaming approval and nodding and gesturing 'quite unaware that every eye in the rustic congregation was fixed upon him'.

This glimpse of his engaging eccentricity is typical of his family life throughout his years of retirement. No account of Wilberforce's life can be complete without an attempt to show him in the midst of his loving family and friends. His had always been a curiously disorganised household. Robert Southey, the poet, tells of a visit to Keswick in 1818. 'Wilberforce has been here with all his household, and such a household! The principle of the family seems to be that, provided the servants have faith, good works are not to be expected from them, and the utter disorder which prevails in consequence is truly farcical. The old coachman would figure upon a stage. . . . I have seen nothing in such pell mell topsy turvy chaotic confusion as Wilberforce's apartments. His wife sits in the midst of it like patience on a monument, and he frisks about as if every vein in his body were filled with quicksilver; but with all, there is such a constant hilarity in every look and motion, such a sweetness in all his tones, such a benignity in all his thoughts, words, and actions, that all sense of his grotesque appearance is presently overcome, and you can feel nothing but love and admiration for a creature of so happy and blessed a nature.'

Southey's observations are borne out by many others. John Colquhoun said that anyone who saw Wilberforce first thing in the morning was especially lucky, 'For the little figure, brandishing his spud (a small digging tool) flew about like a butterfly on a summer's morning, now lighting on a flower, and pointing out its beauties; now watching the flight of an insect, charmed with its movements; . . . then extracting a book from his pocket, which was loaded with volumes that dragged his coat to his heels, he pointed out some lines of poetry or recited them; as the leaf, which marked the passage was swept off by the wind a greater vagrant than himself, he ran to catch it, and failing to recover it, he stooped down to gather other leaves, covering his buttonholes with flowers, talking, gesticulating, listening, bright, volatile and restless as a child. But if his companion dropped a grave remark, or told of some deed of kindness or trait of goodness his face lighted up and his eyes filled with tears, but if he told of evil deeds and evil men, the face became at once over-clouded. . . . After the morning walk the conversation flowed on around the breakfast table, protracted often until noon, nor could anyone break away. For if he were a talker, such a listener he found! . . . So it was that his table always overflowed. To be sure, in the earlier days when the dinner table gathered its crowd of guests at Broomfield or Kensington Gore, it was not easy to find seats or supplies of food or knives and forks. Those whom the butler favoured often had a hint to take their seat early or they would find none. Yet people crowded there despite inconvenience. And his talk, what was it like? . . . like an ethereal essence which fills the atmosphere you enjoy, but can't recall or impart it. Yet one trait was constant, he never gave a wound or left a sting. He never willingly dwelt on evil or the foibles of others. If he could, he passed them by, if pressed on him he spoke of them with reluctance, and was on the watch for some redeeming feature.'

There are numerous accounts like this, many of them emphasising his love of books and his infinite capacity for reading. When he lived in Old Palace Yard he would keep small volumes in every pocket when ever he went into the House and when in the country books and flowers occupied much of his affectionate attention. Long after his retirement from the House, and after many family tragedies and upsets, he was still lively. As late as 1830 we hear of him on a visit, 'Infirm as he is in his advanced years, he flies about with astonishing activity, and while with nimble fingers he seizes upon everything that adorns or diversifies his path, his mind flits from object to object with unceasing versatility. . . . Wilberforce is like a bee, Wilberforce sparkles with life and wit and the characteristic of his mind is rapid productiveness. Wilberforce is always sunshine'.

Writing in the very month of his death one of his friends recalled how whenever he walked about his house, 'he was generally humming the tune of a hymn or psalm as though he could not contain his pleasurable feelings of thankfulness and devotion; nor could we reasonably complain of this custom for his voice at that time was remarkably sweet and melodious.'

Even when real tragedy struck, as when his eldest daughter Lizzie died, he was able to find consolation. 'What a November evening prospect would now lie before me were it not for the flood of light and of life which flows from under the Throne of God and of the Lamb'.

One of those who observed him with most perception and affection was Marianne Thornton, Henry's daughter, who knew him from 1815 until his death. There is a delightful sketch of hers showing him at Battersea Rise, a tiny figure, bent almost double, pouring over a book in the middle of the elegant library which was designed by Pitt. She describes a call he made there in 1825. 'Mr. Wilberforce himself surprised us beyond measure by appearing on our lawn on Monday to pay us a visit and he was strong enough to spend almost the whole of it in walking upon the grass, inhaling, as he said, the gales and roses and listening to the concerts of nightingales. He looks very thin and reduced and walks feebly but really he is almost a proof already of the immortality of the soul, though I never saw him in such spirits or appear so keenly alive upon all subjects'.

She too remarked upon the total disorganisation of his home and how Mrs Wilberforce, 'seems to like this huggar-muggar way of going on', and of the charity which obliged them to keep servants who could be of no possible assistance. 'Things go on in the old way, the house thronged with servants who are all lame or impotent or blind or kept from charity; an ex-secretary kept because he is grateful and his wife because she nursed poor Barbara, and the old butler, who they wish would not stay, but then he is so attached and his wife who was the cook but now she is so infirm. All this is rather as it should be for one likes to see him so completely in character and would willingly sit in despair of getting one's plate changed at dinner, and hear a chorus of bells all day which nobody answers for the sake of seeing Wilberforce in his element.'

What was also endearing about him was his ability to laugh at his own adversities. On the eve of his son's financial catastrophe in dairy farming he was able to say, 'I wish William would keep company with his father instead of his cows. It would be quite as profitable and much more agreeable'.

There is a delightful description too of the family at prayers in 1828. 'The scene at prayers was a most curious one. There is a bell which rings as Mr. Wilberforce begins to dress; another when he finishes dressing; upon which Mr. Barningham begins to play a hymn upon the organ and sing a solo, and by degrees the family come down to the entrance hall . . . first one joins in and then another; Lizzie calling out, "Don't go near Mama, she sings so dreadfully out of tune, dear" and William, "don't look at Papa, he does make such dreadful faces", so he does, waving his arms about and occasionally pulls the leaves off the geraniums and smelling them, singing louder and louder in a tone of hilarity; trust him; praise Him; trust Him; praise Him ever more.'

There is a marvellous endearing dottiness about it all and through every account his love of home and family shines out.

It was so to the very end, though he was buffeted by financial disaster caused by his son's folly and though he suffered grievous bereavement too, especially when Lizzie and his brother-in-law James Stephen, his greatest friend of later years, died. Through it all he kept his serene good humour and his abiding faith.

Although he was out of public life his total devotion to his cause led to his making occasional speeches. He presided at a great meeting of the Anti-Slavery Society in the Freemason's Hall as late as 1830. It was a moving scene as Clarkson, who had himself suffered a breakdown many years previously but had come back to take a prominent role in the movement again, moved that Wilberforce, 'the great leader in our cause', should take the chair. The aim now was the total abolition of slavery and Wilberforce rejoiced when in the General Election of 1830, Yorkshire, now entitled to four members, returned four abolitionists.

His very last public appearance came almost three years later, on April 12th, 1833. He was staying with Robert at East Farley in Kent and went to Maidstone to propose a petition against slavery. He was old and infirm far beyond his years but he addressed his audience with clarity. As he finished speaking he said 'I trust that we have now approached the very end of our career', and then that shaft of sunlight lit up his face and he exclaimed, 'the object is bright before us, the light of Heaven beams upon us, as an earnest of success'.

Four months later Parliament decreed that slavery should be abolished. Wilberforce died within two days of hearing the news.

12

A Place in History

In the House in which Wilberforce was born in Hull there is a museum to his memory and in the birth room the simple inscription, 'Statesman, orator, philanthropist, saint.' In these simple words the citizens of Hull sought to express their pride in Wilberforce's achievements and their assessment of them. How far was that assessment a just one? 150 years after his death should it be echoed or amended?

All public men have their critics and no great man was ever perfect. Wilberforce himself, as we have seen, subjected his own conduct to the most ruthless self-examination throughout his life. Those personal criticisms were not the only, or the most important, that were made of him. We have seen how greatly he was loved and admired by many, but throughout his life his friends gently chided his faults and some formidable critics challenged his opinions, his actions, and even his integrity.

What were these criticisms? How far, if at all, do they invalidate the simple but moving praise of his fellow citizens, or the eloquent eulogy of his epitaph in Westminster Abbey?

'In an age and country fertile in great and good men
He was among the foremost of those who fixed the character of
their times
Because to high and various talents,
To warm benevolence, and to universal candour,
He added the abiding eloquence of a Christian life'

Sir George Stephen, whose admiration for Wilberforce was real and abiding, nevertheless was not blind to his faults. He saw with the charity of a friend, noting that, 'a man's excellence, especially when a public man, cannot be appreciated apart from his failings, as the primary colours lose their brilliance, when deprived of contrast with their complementary tints!' For Stephen, Wilberforce's central fault was 'busy indolence'. This was the essential companion of his butterfly mind. Stephen is fairly severe in his strictures. 'He worked nothing out for himself. he was destitute of system, and desultory in his habits; he depended on others for his information, and laid himself open to misguidance; he was too fond of an animated dictionary; he required an intellectual walking stick. From this habit sprung another failing of no trifling importance in a public man – he was indecisive; he wanted the confidence which he might have justly placed in his own judgment. The common saying of him, so common that you must have heard it, that you might safely predict his vote, for it was certain to be opposed to his speech. The only other weak point to which I shall refer was singular in a man of his refinement – he loved the small gossip of political life and politically educated in the tone of the last century felt, perhaps unconsciously, too much deferential regard for rank and power, irrespective, not of the morality, but of the sterling worth of their possessors'.

His indecisiveness, which could obviously be infuriating, was noted by many commentators during his life. In a series of 'Parliamentary Portraits' produced in 1815 the writer talks of his 'want of decision, arising some think from timidity, others say from want of high-mindedness, which seemed to be his principal foible'.

Stephen saw these human failings as essentially trivial in comparison with his qualities and the author of the profile just quoted thought it 'a humiliation to descend to scan petty defects' in so great a man, asking 'who would estimate Locke by his prolixity or Shakespeare by his puns?'

But these were the judgements of admirers. There were others who were more severe. In an assessment of 'Public Characters 1800–1801' a generally favourable review of his career to date nevertheless was unhappy about his 'Practical View', which the

author alleged was thought 'by many denominations of Christians
. . . to possess but a small share of that spirit of mildness and
charity which is uniformly recommended both in the precepts
and example of their Lord and Master'. And Sydney Smith,
perhaps the Church of England's greatest wit, said of Wilberforce's famous Proclamation Society that it was, 'the Society for the
suppression of Vice among those with less than £500 per year'.

Here, indeed, we are approaching the substance of the more
serious criticisms which were constantly levelled against him
throughout his political life. It was not just those who feared,
however mistakenly, that the abolition of the slave trade would
damage the Navy or colonial wealth who took issue with his
greatest campaign. Nelson might have been guilty of a very real
moral blindness when he wrote about 'the damnable and cursed
doctrines of Wilberforce and his hypocritical allies'.

There was much of special pleading in the West Indian planter
who urged that it would be 'as humane, and a little less pres-
umptuous if they would exert their benevolence at home, and
would not meddle with the Colonies'.

Those were predictable reactions from interested parties but
many of Wilberforce's contemporaries in Britain did think that
it was hypocritical of him to devote so much time to improving
the lot of people he had never seen, in countries of which he
knew little and of concentrating on seeking to reform the morals
of his own fellow citizens, whilst not engaging in more active
campaigns of social reform in Britain.

William Cobbett, radical campaigner and an idealist with no
time for Christianity, loathed Wilberforce. At the time of the
climax of the campaign against abolition Cobbett declared, 'So
often as they agitate this question, with all its cant, the relief of
500,000 blacks; so often will I remind them of the one million
two hundred thousand white paupers in England and Wales'.
Fifteen years later Cobbett was even more vitriolic when he
talked of 'the labourers' bill of fayre in the glorious times of high
prices; a gallon loaf and three pence a week for each person in
a labourer's family! – that is to say about 18 ounces of bread a
day, no meat and nothing else for food, and THREE PENCE to
find a drink, clothing, washing, fire, light and lodging for the

week! Gracious God! And this is England! And was this what
was allowed by English magistrates to English labourers in hus-
bandry! And at this very moment was Mr. Wilberforce receiving
the incessant plaudits for his humane exertions in favour of the
black slaves in the Colonies! And did he never utter one word on
behalf of the poor creatures, the wretched human beings of
Wiltshire? . . .'

The less excitable and more balanced essayist William Hazlitt
made similar criticism in 'The Spirit of the Age', published in
1825. He accused Wilberforce of acting from mixed motives. 'He
would willingly serve two masters, God and Mammon. He is a
person of many excellent and admirable qualifications, but he
has made a mistake in wishing to reconcile those that are incompatible. He has a most winning eloquence, specious, persuasive,
familiar, silver-tongued. He is amiable, charitable, conscientious,
pious, loyal, humane, attractable to power, and accessible to
popularity, honouring the King, and no less charmed with the
homage of his fellow citizens. 'What lacks he then? Nothing but
an economy of good parts. By aiming at too much he has spoilt
all and neutralised what might have been an estimable character,
distinguished by single services to mankind. A man must make
his choice not only between virtue and vice, but between different
virtues. Otherwise he will not gain his own approbation or secure
the respect of others. . . .' He accused Wilberforce of seeking to
be all things to all men, anxious to have the praise of everyone.
'We suspect he is not quite easy in his mind because West Indian
planters and Guinea traders do not join in his praise'. He accused
him of turning a blind eye towards the 'claims set up by the
despots of the earth over their continental subjects.'

According to Hazlitt, 'his patriotism, his philanthropy are not
so ill-bred as to quarrel with his loyalties or to banish him from
the first circles. He preaches vital Christianity to untutored sav-
ages; and tolerates its worst abuses in civilised states. . . . There
is in all this a good deal of the appearance of cant and tricking.
He has two strings to his bow – he by no means neglects his
worldly interests, while he expects a bright reversion in the skies.
Mr. Wilberforce is far from being a hypocrite; but he is, we
think, as fine a specimen of moral equivocation as can well be

conceived. He carefully chooses his grounds to fight the battles of loyalty, religion, and humanity, and it is such as is always safe and advantageous to himself! . . .' For Hazlitt the real hero of abdication was Clarkson and not Wilberforce.

These are serious criticisms made by serious men and they cannot lightly be brushed aside. But they do not stand up to the closest scrutiny.

To understand Wilberforce we have to accept that he was a man of his time. He took for granted the basic social structure and many of the social conventions of the late 18th century. As we have seen in this short account of his life, he did work energetically for, and give generously to, campaigns and organisations aimed at improving the lot of the poor. But he believed that the best chance for a secure and stable future for his country depended upon a maintenance of social stability and he was genuinely concerned lest the upheavals of France should be repeated in England. He was concerned because of the bloodshed and chaos which might accompany them; because of the threat they posed to the Parliamentary system and, far more important even than that, because they would imperil the Christian religion. It could be argued that Wilberforce's reputation has suffered because of the inevitable and proper association of his name with the triumphant campaign against the slave trade. The fact is that he was highly regarded in his own time, not just because he campaigned with such persistence and eloquence on that issue, and not just because he sought to turn the minds and lives of his countrymen towards a more religious life, but, because, as a Christian Politician, he sought to bring his judgement to bear upon all of the great issues of the day.

The charge of indecisiveness is, up to a point, a reasonable one. But his was the indecisiveness of the true independent who genuinely tried to view each issue on its merits. He viewed it, nevertheless, from the standpoint of an English gentleman who wanted to preserve the fabric and stability of the State. For us to criticise Wilberforce for seeking to uphold the monarchy would be as sensible as for an American to criticise George Washington for wanting to institute a Republic. Destruction of one system was incompatible with the achievement of Wilberforce's aims, just as the creation of the other system was essential to the achievement of Washington's.

As Wilberforce saw it, there could be no spiritual regeneration without social stability and we can detect this as a constant theme throughout his interventions in Parliament on all of the great issues of the day.

It was what made him challenge, from time to time, the necessity of continuing the war against France. Every effort should be made to achieve peace, he said in 1795, not least because 'one bad effect of the war was, the drawing off of so many of the people to a military life. This was a very serious evil, tending to hurt essentially the morals of the people and to detach them from the habits of civil life; and though no present consequences might be felt, yet very material ones might at some distance of time follow'.

But he was no pacifist and when overtures for peace were unsuccessful he gave Pitt total support in prosecuting the war. He was also prepared to give support in time of war to unpleasant domestic measures if he thought them essential for maintaining security and unity at home. Thus, again in 1795, he spoke out forcefully in favour of the Seditious Meetings Bill. Bad men, he said, 'were trying to excite contempt for the British constitution and an attachment to those false principles of liberty, which had produced such extensive mischiefs in a neighbouring country. He noted their marked contempt for everything sacred, an avowed opposition to the religion, as well as the constitution, of Great Britain.' Not that he ever found supporting such Measures easy: 'He was ready to confess that it was not willingly that he resorted to this Bill; all that was left to him was a choice of difficulties.'

It was because he appreciated the practicalities of politics that he spoke out in 1808 against Henry Grattan's attempt at Roman Catholic Emancipation, because he felt, 'that to grant the Catholics their present claim would by no means satisfy them completely', and because 'with respect to the time, I do not think the present a proper one, if there were no other reason that it is impossible now to carry the Measure.' He was obviously particularly unhappy in this opposition. He had supported Emancipation

before and five years later he was speaking out firmly for it again
saying that it appeared to him to be absurd to prevent Catholics
from holding seats in the House. 'It has been objected the Catholics might form mischievous or treasonable connections with foreign powers, but the connection existed now; and while
concession would not increase the connection with a foreign
power it would render the influence of that power less effective.'
Again we see the practical politician as well as the idealist.

We do not have to agree with everything that Wilberforce said
to acknowledge that he was trying to be just and trying to be
practical, just as when, in 1815, he supported the Corn Bill which
levied a high duty on imported wheat. Whilst he expressed great
sympathy with those who were worried at the price of bread, he
felt that a thriving agriculture was essential and he believed that
the Bill would, 'afford a sufficient inducement to the agricultural-
ist to improve his land, because he knew his expense would be
repaid by it.' And so 'because the lower price was likely to
diminish the cultivation of land, he thought it might produce an
injury to the country that would be terrible to contemplate. On
this head, one side was as much concerned as the other – the
consumer as much as the grower. . . . Having, therefore, come
to this conclusion, he felt it his urgent, though painful duty,
under the present circumstances, to vote in favour of the
Measure.'

He approached the question of the Habeas Corpus Suspension
Bill in 1817 in much the same spirit. Although reluctant to
approve of the suspension of so important a privilege he would
support the Measure, but only so long as the Ministers deemed
it necessary for the safety of the country. Always fearful of social
revolution Wilberforce would 'readily conceive how the lower
orders . . . might be tempted by the delusive and wicked principles instilled into their minds, to direct their strength to the
destruction of Governments and to the overthrow of every civil
and religious establishment'. He accepted that there was a pos-
sibility that the Measure might be abused but 'it was often the
accident of human affairs, that nothing was left but a choice of
evil, and such he conceived to be now the case. . . . He certainly
thought it an evil; at the same time he hoped the natural good

sense of the people of England would at length restore them to
their suspended rights. Till then he must, for the sake of the
patient poor, for the sake even of the turbulent themselves,
consent to the passing of the Bill now proposed'.

At the same time, indeed in the very same year, he was prepared to speak out against the Game Laws because he believed
that they were unjust, subjecting 'individuals to a severe penalty
for an act which it was contrary to the natural feeling of mankind
to say was in itself a crime'. And in 1819 he talked of the Game
Laws as being 'so opposite to every principle of personal liberty,
so contrary to all our notions of private right, so injurious, so
arbitrary in their operation that the sense of the greater part of
mankind was in determined hostility to them'. So it was that,
again behaving as a practical politician, he argued for the introduction of Game Licences so that 'no person should be allowed
to sell game who did not have a licence for that purpose, such
licences to be granted by the Magistrates'. By this means he
believed that poaching, an important source of supply to satisfy
the enormous demand for game, would effectively be outlawed.

It is always easy to look back upon a time when attitudes were
different from what they are today and to condemn with hindsight. Today, sadly, there are probably far fewer in this country,
where so many faiths are practised and where a small minority
of nominal Christians attend any place of worship, who would
feel total sympathy for Wilberforce's fierce desire to bring the
benefits of Christianity to others. We get a clear insight into his
views on this matter from a speech he made during a debate on
the Propagation of Christianity in India. He devoutly believed
that the people of the Sub Continent must not be denied access
to the one true Faith. 'Blest be God, we have a remedy fully
adequate, and specially appropriate to the purpose. That remedy,
Sir, is Christianity, which I justly call the appropriate remedy;
for Christianity then assumes her true character, no less than she
performs her natural and proper office, when she takes under her
protection those poor degraded beings on whom philosophy looks
down with disdain, or perhaps with contemptuous condescen-
sion. On the first promulgation of Christianity it was declared by
its great Author as "Glad Tidings to the Poor" and ever faithful

to her character, Christianity still delights to instruct the ignorant, succour the needy, to comfort the sorrowful, to visit the
foresaken.'

It was this belief above all others that governed his life and
motivated his every action, but it would be doing Wilberforce a
great dis-service merely to acknowledge him as 'a Christian politician'. For his influence stemmed not only from his belief but
from his quality of mind. It was a quality that was recognised
from the time when he first went into the House and when he
was the closest confidante of the Prime Minister, Pitt, to the eve
of his retirement, almost half a century later, when his parliamentary colleagues asked him to seek to mediate in the quarrel
between George IV and his Queen, Caroline, in a vain attempt
to prevent an unseemly public recital of events which would be,
as Wilberforce himself had prophesied, 'Long, painful, and
disgusting'.

Throughout his life Wilberforce did what he thought was
necessary for his country's good. All his actions were coloured
by his ideal of a politically stable country where men in high
places and in low would turn increasingly to the Christian Gospel
for guidance and refreshment. He fixed upon the slave trade, the
subject of his greatest campaign, because he did not believe that
any country could ever profess and call itself Christian while it
condoned the trade. Perhaps there were times when his devotion
to this cause, and his obsession with the need to defeat the
enemies of religion, made him blind to those social evils in his
own country which others more readily identified. But no one
who has any experience of public life can really support or sustain
a criticism of a public figure which is based on the accusation
that he did not, in every issue, see the truth or fight against evil.

Statesman, orator – no one could seriously deny Wilberforce
either title. His philanthrophy was evident not only in his financial generosity to a multitude of 'good causes' but in that love
of his fellow men revealed in so many little things, such as his
unwillingness to wound in debate, even though he had a powerful
gift of invective.

Was he a saint? If a saint is a man who devotes his life to
seeking to serve his Maker wholeheartedly and bends all his

talents to causes which would advance Christian brotherhood and love, Wilberforce certainly qualified.

One thing above all others shines out from every account by those who knew him: he was the most loveable of men. He was a man of real charm and true grace, in the social as well as the religious sense, and a man, moreover, who was full of fun, who could not only catalogue his own faults, but laugh at them. Wherever he went he generated gaiety and that was as true after his conversion as it was when he kept his pie in his rooms in Cambridge to share in the small hours with any companion who could be tempted to talk through to the dawn.

Of all the great figures of the last two centuries whose names come most readily to mind, few are politicians. Those who are do so not only because of their abilities but because they held high office in difficult times. Wilberforce alone is remembered simply because he did great good. Any Christian politician must be inspired by the thought that he did it because he tried to follow his Master.

Further Reading

By far the best modern biography of Wilberforce is that by Robin Furneaux (Hamish Hamilton, 1974). John Pollock's Wilberforce (Constable, 1976) is also a very readable and enjoyable 'life'.

Anyone who becomes totally absorbed in the study of this most fascinating of men would want to read Professor Coupland's life, first published in 1923 and reissued in 1945.

The monumental life by Robert and Samuel Wilberforce and their edited edition of his letters also make rewarding reading.

The best study of the slave trade is Roger Anstey's "The Atlantic Slave Trade and British Abolition, 1760 to 1810" (Macmillan, 1975).

Those interested in the history of the period in general should consult the appropriate volumes in the "Oxford History of England", J. Stephen Watson's "The Reign of George III" and E. L. Woodward's "The Age of Reform". Both volumes have extensive bibliographies, as do Furneaux's and Pollock's biographies.

Index